Easy-to-make
Furniture

By the Editors of Sunset Books

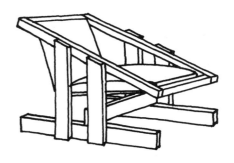

Lane Publishing Co. • Menlo Park, California

Foreword

Anyone—including you—can make stylish, comfortable furniture. Just take the time and invest in the tools; this book will give you the plans and guidance you need. It will show you how to create pride-inspiring furniture quickly and easily.

In the book, you'll find furniture to fill nearly every need: shelving, chairs, couches, tables, desks, bedroom furniture, children's furniture, outdoor furniture—even a sewing center, a wine rack, and a bar. The pieces are simple, functional, contemporary, and relatively inexpensive to make.

For their help, we would like to thank Art Center College of Design; George Dean of Mobilia; Bill Hull; Joyce, Lever & Rogers; The Just Plain Smith Company; Frank Lucas Woodworking; Patterns Ltd.; R & E Designs; Ron Rezek; Satisfaction—Promise Custom Woodworking; Warren Shaw; Earle T. Stebben; Sullivan Canvas; Roberta Vandervort; and Weingarten Stereo.

Edited by Donald W. Vandervort

Design and Illustrations: Joe Seney

Photography: Norman A. Plate

Cover: Shelving system directions on page 7; chair directions on page 24; coffee table directions on page 21.

Editor, Sunset Books: David E. Clark

First Printing May 1977

Contents

Particle board chair *is easy to make; handy pouches in backrest store magazines. See page 23.*

QUICK & EASY FURNITURE

. . . from not-so-raw materials

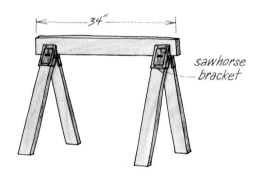

Door-and-Sawhorses Dining Table

Construction requires a 3' by 6'8" hollow-core door, two sawhorses 29" tall, wood sealer, and enamel paint. Design: Christy Higgins

Wire Ice-cream Baskets

Purchased at a dairy or from someone who specializes in recycling such materials, these baskets make interesting, inexpensive shelving. You might try the same idea with other types of baskets or boxes.

Jeans Pockets Storage

Recycled denim pockets, nailed to a plywood sheet with carpet tacks, make an interesting wall organizer. If you don't want to cut up your friendly old jeans, pick some up at a secondhand store. Design: Roberta Vandervort

Cushion Seating

Stack up cushions and secure them with elastic belts for a comfy seat. When you want informal seating for three, unbelt and scatter them.

Bolt-together Shelving

Bolted joints are sturdy, easy to assemble.
See facing page.
Design: Donald Wm. MacDonald, AIA

Upholstered Wall System

Hingeless doors adhere with
hook-and-pile tape.
See page 8.
Design: Craig Hanson

STORAGE SYSTEMS

One displays collectables, the other conceals clutter

Bolt-together Shelving

Photos on facing page

A stack of plywood rectangles, a couple of dozen short 2 by 2s, and umpteen nuts and bolts can turn a messy room into an organized one.

For practically any room—child's room, recreation room, office, bedroom, living room—this versatile system can solve your storage problems. Why is it so versatile? Primarily because you can make it nearly any size. It's modular. Just figure the size and shape that best suit your situation and bolt the boards together.

TOOLS YOU'LL NEED: pencil · measuring tape · square · handsaw · drill · 5/16" bit · adjustable wrench · pliers · sandpaper and finishing tools. *Helpful tools* include a radial-arm or table saw, drill press, power sander, and socket set.

MATERIALS LIST (for the unit shown):
36' of 2 by 2 (1½" by 1½" alder is shown)
2 sheets of ¾" A-A (or birch) plywood
1 box (100) hex-head bolts, ¼" by 2½"
1 box (100) hex-head bolts, ¼" by 3½"
2 boxes (200) nuts, ¼"
About 275 washers, ¼"
Wood filler
White enamel paint

HERE'S HOW

First cut each sheet of plywood into 24 equal pieces, each 12" by 16" (minus the width of the saw cuts). To simplify your work, you may wish to have lumberyard personnel make the long rip cuts.

Next, cut the 2 by 2 bars to length. You can either cut them 12" long and leave the ends square, or you can cut them 13" long and trim the ends, as shown in drawing 7-1.

When drilling the holes, you'll have to do precise work. Carefully mark the holes on one 2 by 2 as shown in drawing 7-2. Then drill the holes straight (see page 70 for

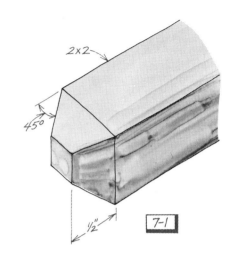

7-1

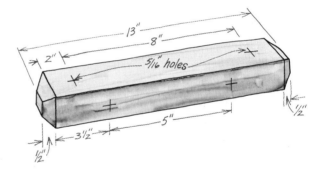

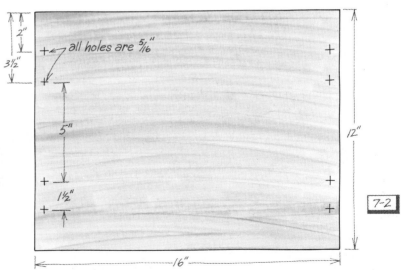

7-2

hints on drilling straight). Use this 2 by 2 as a guide for drilling all the plywood pieces and for starting the holes in the other 2 by 2s. (After you've drilled the first hole in each, drop a bolt in to keep the guide 2 by 2 from moving as you drill the second hole.)

Fill the plywood edges with wood filler, and sand them flat. Then refill and sand again. Repeat until you're satisfied that they're good and flat. Then apply two coats of enamel to the plywood. For this, you can use a brush, a roller (this goes faster), or—for a really professional finish—a sprayer.

When the paint is dry, you're ready to begin assembling the unit. Use the long bolts where two panels join to opposite sides of a 2 by 2; use the short bolts where only one panel joins a 2 by 2. Refer to our photograph of the unit to help keep the assembly simple, unless you wish to customize it for your room. It pays to have a friend help during assembly—in fact, invite several and make a party of it.

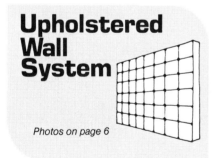

Upholstered Wall System

Photos on page 6

Imagine a marshmallow wall that devours all the clutter in a room. That's what this soft, padded wall system is: a shelving unit that puts all your books, papers, magazines, slides—you name it— out of view.

And you don't have to hang a hinge to make it. It's built primarily from plywood, with fabric-and-foam-covered doors that cling to the cabinet fronts with claws of hook-and-pile sewing tape.

TOOLS YOU'LL NEED: pencil · measuring tape · square · radial-arm or table saw · drill · 5⁄16" bit · hammer · nailset (or large nail) · stapling gun · screwdriver · pliers · scissors · serrated bread knife. *Helpful tools* include an electric carving knife and a dado blade.

MATERIALS LIST:
5 sheets of ½" A-D plywood
6 sheets of ¼" A-D plywood
8 machine bolts, ¼" by 2", with nuts
16 washers, ¼"
1-pound box of 4d finishing nails
1-pound box of 6d finishing nails
1 box of 7⁄16" staples
White glue
Wood filler
1 square yard of illustration board
150 square feet of foam, ½" thick
15 yards of fabric, 54" wide
200" of sewing hook-and-pile tape

HERE'S HOW

For a clear understanding of the construction of this shelving system, you should first recognize that it is actually three separate cabinets butted together. The two outside cabinets are each 45" wide; the center cabinet is 30" wide. Though the materials listed for this project will make a system like the one shown in the photograph on page 6, you can make whatever number of units you want.

Begin by cutting the plywood sheets. From three of the ¼"-thick sheets, cut the cabinet backs. Two are 45" by 90"; one is 30" by 90". From the remainder of the sheet the smaller back came from, and from the other three full sheets of ¼" plywood, cut forty-eight 14½" squares for the doors. You'll have a large remainder from one of these sheets that you can use for extra shelves or for another project.

Rip each of four ½"-thick plywood sheets into four 10" by 96" panels, setting the waste aside. From the 10" panels, cut six 90" pieces for the sides, fourteen 44½" pieces for the long shelves and tops, and seven 29½" pieces for the short shelves and top. From the ½"-thick waste pieces and from the fifth ½"-thick plywood sheet, rip eleven 3" by 90" strips and fifty-six 3" by 11" strips for the front face frame of the cabinets.

Drawing 8-1 shows one of the three cabinets that make up the system shown in the photograph on page 6. Because construction techniques for all three cabinets are identical, the following instructions discuss only the 30" cabinet.

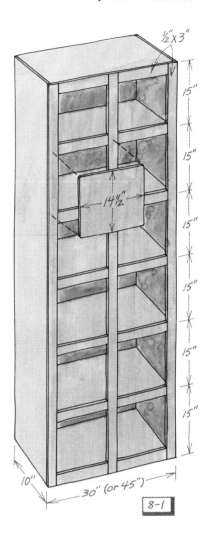

For the other two, duplicate the procedures but make the cabinets 45" wide.

First cut the rabbet and dado grooves in the side pieces, as detailed in drawing 9-1. For this cutting, a dado blade on a radial-arm or table saw works best (for more about cutting grooves, see page 68).

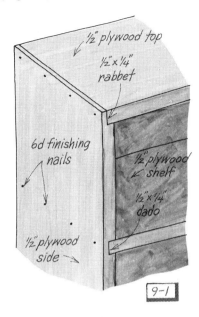

Assemble the sides and shelves by squirting glue in the grooves, pushing the shelf ends into the grooves, and nailing through the sides, into the shelf ends with 6-penny finishing nails. As you nail, use a square to check all of the angles of the shelves to the sides, keeping them perpendicular. Set the nail heads slightly below the surface.

Glue and nail the plywood back to the assembly of sides and shelves. Use 4-penny nails. If cut properly, the back should square up the cabinet.

Now add the vertical face-frame strips to the unit's front, gluing them and nailing with 6-penny finishing nails. Use the same method to attach the horizontal strips (see drawing 9-2). Check them with a square to be sure they're perpendicular to the vertical strips.

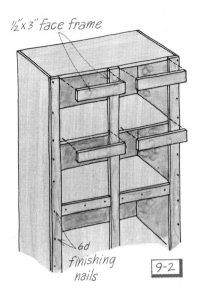

Set all nail heads below the surface and apply wood filler. Sand the face frame, rounding its edges slightly. Reapply filler and sand again if necessary.

Now for the doors. Use a serrated bread knife or an electric carving knife to cut the forty-eight 17" squares of foam. Then, with scissors, cut forty-eight 18" squares of fabric.

To cover each door, wrap a foam square around a plywood square, stretching the foam slightly and folding the corners into miters, as shown in drawing 9-3. Staple

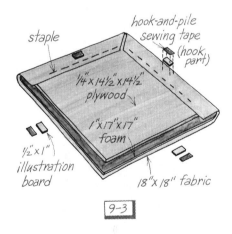

around the perimeter of the foam edges. Then wrap fabric around the foam, carefully folding the corners, and staple the fabric edges to the door's backside.

Cut pieces of foam for the cabinet sides that will be visible, and for the cabinet's top if it will be in view. Do not upholster any cabinet side that will butt against another. Attach the

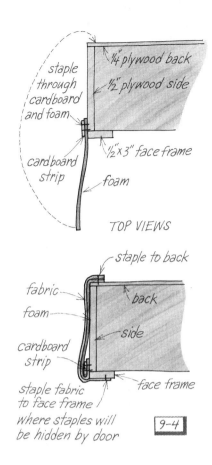

TOP VIEWS

foam as shown in drawing 9-4. Cut fabric and attach it over the foam as shown in the same drawing.

Staple ½" by 1" pieces of illustration board to the backside of each door, in the locations shown in drawing 9-3. To each piece, glue a 1" strip of the hook part of hook-and-pile sewing tape. Apply the other half to the corresponding locations on the shelving unit.

When you've made all three cabinet units, stand them up in place. Butt together the sides that are not upholstered, and be sure the slight gaps between them are uniform. Drill a ⁵⁄₁₆" hole through the side of one cabinet and into the adjoining cabinet, and bolt the two together with ¼" bolts, putting washers on both sides. Use four bolts—two high and two low—to join each pair of units.

Push the doors in place to complete your upholstered wall system.

STEREO CENTER

Sleek, contemporary cabinet for stereo gear

Handsome redwood and acrylic plastic give this stereo center its character. Earthy warmth comes from the redwood; the plastic dust cover offers sleek, contemporary styling.

The unit's compartments holds a tuner-amplifier, a record turntable, and a cassette tape deck. Along the trestle base there's plenty of storage space for records and tapes.

Though the directions and materials list given are for making the unit shown, you can alter the compartment sizes to fit your stereo components.

TOOLS YOU'LL NEED: pencil · measuring tape · square · radial-arm or table saw · rasp · drill · ⅜" and 1" bits, #8 by 1¼" and #8 by 1¾" screw pilots · hammer · nailset (or large nail) · screwdriver · Allen wrenches · ⁹⁄₁₆" socket and handle · bar or pipe clamps · sandpaper and finishing tools. *Helpful tools* include a drill press, a router, and a power sander.

MATERIALS LIST:

All redwood specified is graded Clear, all-heart.
3' of 2 by 2 redwood
16' of 2 by 4 redwood
5' of 2 by 6 redwood
17' of 1 by 12 redwood
12' of 1 by 10 redwood
4' of 1 by 8 redwood
5' of ¼" by ¾" redwood molding
½ sheet (24" by 96") of ¼" pegboard
4 Allen-head bolts, ⅜" by 2"
4 Allen-head bolts, ⅜" by 3½"
4 Allen-head bolts, ⅜" by 7"
24 washers, ⅜"
12 nuts, ⅜"
4 flathead screws, 1¼" by #8
8 flathead screws, 1¾" by #8
1-pound box of 4d finishing nails
2 cedar chest lid support hinges
¼" sheet of smoked acrylic plastic, 18⅛" by 25¾"
U-shaped cupboard handle
Wood filler (redwood)
White glue
Danish oil

HERE'S HOW

Cut and drill the various pieces as specified in drawings 10-1 and 10-2. (For more about the techniques for cutting and drilling, see pages 67 and 70.)

Bolt holes are ⅜". All bolt heads, nuts, and washers are countersunk. Counterbore ⅝" deep with a 1" bit for them.

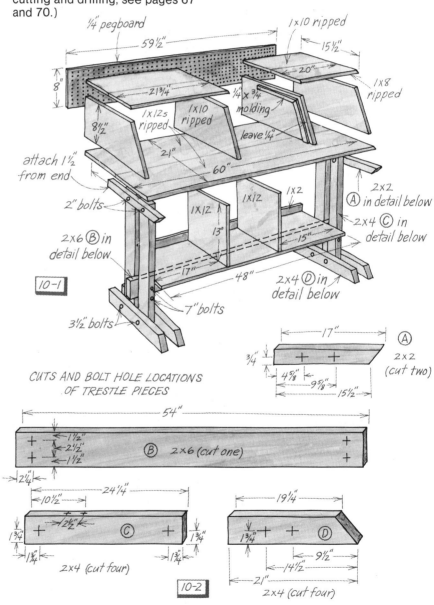

CUTS AND BOLT HOLE LOCATIONS OF TRESTLE PIECES

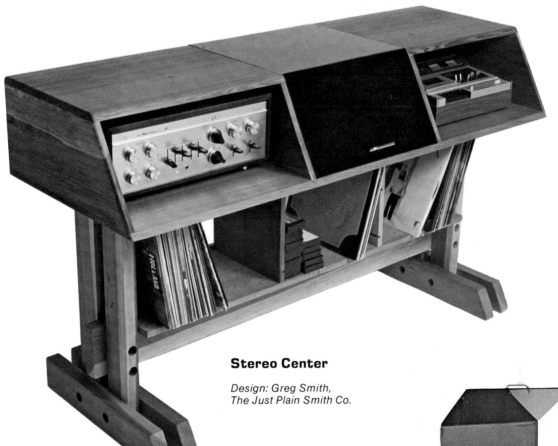

Stereo Center

Design: Greg Smith,
The Just Plain Smith Co.

Dust cover, an optional feature,
is formed from acrylic plastic.

For making the compartments, you must rip the various boards on a radial-arm or table saw. Refer to drawing 10-1 for sizes. Assemble the compartments by gluing along the edges and clamping with bar or pipe clamps. Protect the tender redwood by slipping wood scraps beneath the jaws of the clamps. Wipe off excess glue before it dries.

Round off the compartments' edges with a rasp or router, and then sand until smooth. Attach the pegboard back, using 1¼" screws. You can drill larger holes through the back for stereo wires if necessary.

Assemble the record shelf as shown in drawing 10-1, using glue and 4-penny finishing nails.

Now bolt together the trestle base, referring to drawing 10-1. When you've completed this step, set the compartment on top of the trestle base, centered and located as specified in the drawing, and attach it to each 2 by 2 with two 1¾" screws.

Next, using four 1¾" screws,

fasten the record shelf to the 2 by 6 of the trestle base. Then nail down through the compartment's base into the ends of the upright record dividers, using 4-penny finishing nails. Set the nail heads and fill the nail holes.

Fill any other nail holes or mistakes and sand the unit. Apply two coats of Danish oil.

The dust cover is optional, depending upon whether or not your turntable has one. To make it, first nail the ¼" by ¾" molding in place, as shown in drawing 10-1.

For bending the plastic, buy or borrow a strip heating element from your plastics dealer. (To locate a dealer, look in the Yellow Pages under "Plastics—Rods, Tubes, Sheets.") Heat the plastic sheet until it softens along the line where you intend to bend it. Then set it quickly in place and bend it to the proper curvature, holding it there until it cools and hardens. For further specialized information about cutting or bending acrylic plastics, consult your dealer.

Attach the plastic dust cover to the compartment with lid support hinges as shown in drawing 11-1. Last, add the cupboard handle to the dust cover.

MATCHING GROUP

Furniture from 2 by 2s and dowels

By drilling 2 by 2s and doweling them together, you can make the framework for an entire group of furniture. Shown here are a dining chair, a lounge chair, and a two-level table. You can either copy these directly or let them spark your imagination to create other pieces.

Though the 2 by 2s used for the furniture shown are actually 1½" by 1½" birch, you could select another hardwood or even a strong softwood such as Douglas fir.

For maximum comfort, the dining chair's back could either be lowered or angled. To angle the back, substitute 2 by 4 material for the 2 by 2 back legs and modify dowel placements as shown in detail drawing 12-1.

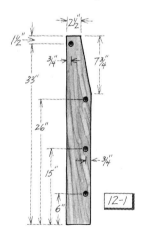

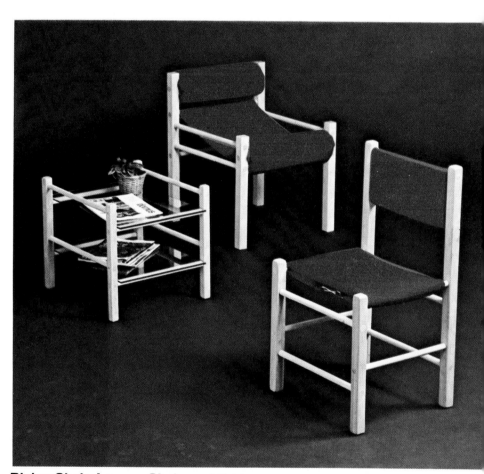

Dining Chair, Lounge Chair, and Table   *Design: Donald Wm. MacDonald, AIA*

TOOLS YOU'LL NEED: *To make any of the pieces* you'll need a pencil, measuring tape, square, handsaw, drill, 1" or expansive bit, hammer or mallet, sandpaper, and finishing tools. *For either chair* you'll need sewing equipment and a serrated bread knife or an electric carving knife. *For the lounge chair* you'll also need a ¼" bit. *Helpful tools* for all pieces include a radial-arm or table saw, drill press, lathe, and power sander.

MATERIALS LIST FOR DINING CHAIR:

10' of 1½" by 1½" birch
17' of 1" doweling
White glue
Wood filler
Clear polyurethane finish
1 block medium foam, 1" by 16" by 10"
1 block medium foam, 1" by 13" by 34"
1⅔ yards of chair canvas
Matching polyester thread
23 grommets, ⅜", with 20' of lacing cord

MATERIALS LIST FOR LOUNGE CHAIR:

9' of 1½" by 1½" birch
16' of 1" doweling
2' of ¼" doweling
White glue
Wood filler
Clear polyurethane finish
2 foam rolls, 6" diameter by 18" long
3 yards of chair canvas
Matching polyester thread
2 yards of drawstring

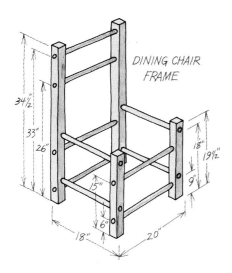

DINING CHAIR FRAME

$34\frac{1}{2}$"
33"
26"
18"
$19\frac{1}{2}$"
9"
15"
6"
18"
20"

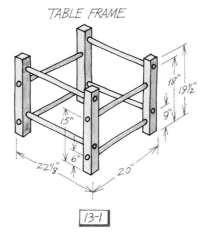

TABLE FRAME

18"
$19\frac{1}{2}$"
9"
15"
6"
$22\frac{1}{8}$"
20"

13-1

LOUNGE CHAIR FRAME

removable $\frac{1}{4}$" dowel pins

26"
21"
29"
13"
19"
21"
15"
17"
$24\frac{1}{2}$"
$22\frac{1}{2}$"

MATERIALS FOR TABLE:

7' of $1\frac{1}{2}$" by $1\frac{1}{2}$" birch
15' of 1" doweling
White glue
Wood filler
Clear polyurethane finish
2 pieces of $\frac{1}{4}$" glass, 17" by 24", edges finished

HERE'S HOW

Often a 1" dowel isn't *exactly* 1", or it isn't perfectly round. Either situation can cause problems in making this furniture. When you drill a 1" hole, you may not be able to get the dowel into it. And if you force it, you may split away the wood on the hole's backside. To avoid this, you can do either of two things: wrap sandpaper around a short length of $\frac{3}{8}$" doweling and sand the hole until the dowel fits, or sand the dowel ends (or turn them on a lathe) until they fit.

To minimize the effect of this problem, you can change the design by drilling the holes only 1" deep instead of all the way through the birch pieces, and cutting an extra inch off the dowel lengths. (Don't make this change on the removable dowels of the lounge chair; they must go all the way through so you can get them out. For these, sand the holes only.)

Cut the dowels and the $1\frac{1}{2}$" by $1\frac{1}{2}$" birch pieces to length according to drawing 13-1. Mark and drill the holes; if you don't have a drill press

for this, exercise your best talents for drilling them straight so the chair will fit together properly. (For hints on drilling, see page 70.)

Sand the holes or dowel ends until the dowels fit snugly. On the lounge chair, don't glue the removable dowels; instead, fasten them by drilling a $\frac{1}{4}$" hole through the leg and dowel and inserting a $1\frac{1}{2}$" length of $\frac{1}{4}$" doweling.

Glue and join with dowels the two front legs, then the two back legs, and finally the front legs to the back. To get the pieces onto the dowel ends, you may need to use a mallet or a hammer and wood block (the block is to protect the birch).

Set the frame on a flat surface, both to make sure that all pieces fit squarely together and to check the frame for wobble. Make any necessary adjustments, wipe off excess glue, and let the glue dry.

Sand, fill any defects, and sand again. Apply two coats of clear polyurethane.

For the table tops, simply set the glass in place on the dowels.

For the dining chair seat and back, make the slings as specified

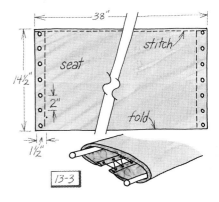

38"
stitch
seat
fold
$14\frac{1}{2}$"
2"
$1\frac{1}{2}$"

13-3

in drawings 13-2 and 13-3. (For more about sewing slings, see page 76.)

For the lounge chair seat and back, you'll have to run two of the removable dowels through the foam rolls. To make holes through the foam, cut the rolls in half lengthwise with a bread knife or an electric carving knife, remove a V-shaped section about 1" deep along the center of each half, and glue the halves back together. Cover the rolls with drawstring covers (page

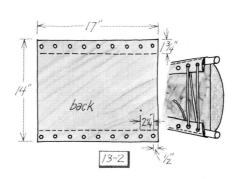

17"
$\frac{3}{4}$"
back
14"
$2\frac{1}{4}$"
$\frac{1}{2}$"

13-2

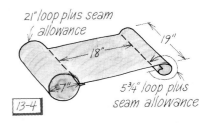

21" loop plus seam allowance
19"
18"
7"
$5\frac{3}{4}$" loop plus seam allowance

13-4

78) and sew a loop sling for the seat as shown in drawing 13-4. (For more about sewing loops, see page 76.)

Modular Corner Couch   *See facing page. Design: Penelope De Paoli/Space Planning/Interior Design*

Oak Butcher Block Couch

See page 16.
Design: Christy Higgins,
Whisler Patri Architects

COUCHES

These two modular styles have oak bases

Modular Corner Couch

Photo on facing page

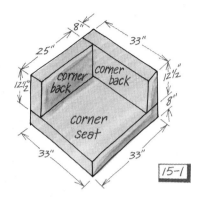

`15-1`

Does your living room have a corner that's perfectly suited for a corner couch? If so, this couch is for you. No matter what length the intersecting walls are, this modular couch can fit them perfectly. You can make it any size—for seating just a few, or for a large group.

Though construction is basic, the couch can require a lot of work, depending on what size you make it.

TOOLS YOU'LL NEED: pencil · measuring tape · square · straightedge (or chalk line) · handsaw · plane · file · drill · #6 by 1¼" pilot bit · hammer · nailset (or large nail) · screwdriver · sandpaper and finishing tools · sewing equipment and sewing machine · serrated bread knife. *Helpful tools* include a miter box; a radial-arm saw, table saw, or power circular saw; a sander; and an electric carving knife.

ABOUT MATERIALS:

Because this couch can be made practically any size, the project doesn't lend itself to a materials list. Instead, figure your material needs from the following information.

Measure the walls where you plan to put the couch to determine the distance you want it to extend in each direction.

Refer to drawing 15-1. There you will see that no matter how long your couch is in either direction, for proper comfort, the corner seat cushion should be 33" by 33", and the corner back cushions should be sized as shown. All cushions are 8" thick; all seat cushions are 33" deep; and all back cushions are 12½" high. These are constants.

The quantities that vary with couch length are the number and width of the other seat and back cushions. To determine the widths of these seat and back cushions, subtract 33" (the corner cushion) from the total length you want each side of the couch to be; then divide by the number of seat cushions you plan to have (the minimum recommended width is about 24").

See the chart on page 16 for help in calculating necessary amounts of cushion materials.

To calculate materials for the base, study drawing 15-2 and expand the various parts to the size of your couch.

When you're buying materials, remember to get 1¼" by #6 screws, glue, wood filler, and Danish oil finish.

HERE'S HOW

Refer to drawing 15-2 for the wood construction specifications. Notice that the front of the couch as shown is 6½" tall; the back is 6". Though this slight slope adds to comfort, it isn't mandatory. If you'd rather not go to the added work of tapering the end pieces, flatten out the seat by making both front and back 6½" tall.

Make the platform before the cushions, gluing and nailing the pieces as shown below.

(Continued on page 16)

`15-2`

. . . Continued from page 15

Glue and screw the 1" by 2" oak trim pieces along the plywood's front and visible end edges, as illustrated in drawing 16-1. Miter them at the corners. Then, from the inside, screw the larger oak boards to the front and the ends that will show. (See drawing 15-2 on page 15.)

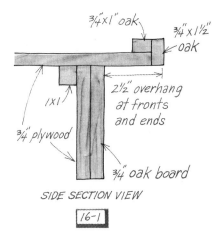

SIDE SECTION VIEW

16-1

Round off visible edges and corners of the oak with a file. Sand, fill any defects or holes, and sand again. Apply two coats of Danish oil finish.

After figuring the finished sizes of the cushions, use the chart above to calculate pattern sizes. The outside cover of each cushion has five pattern pieces: a top, a bottom, a band, and two zipper strips (see drawing 16-2). All patterns allow

for ½" seams. After cutting out the pieces, mark them with corresponding identification numbers to avoid mixing them up while you're making the cushions.

To facilitate removing the outer covers for dry cleaning or washing, make a simple muslin inner covering for the stuffing of each cushion. For the inner covering, follow the directions on page 78 for box cushions. Slip-stitch the openings closed instead of using zippers.

To make the outer covers, cut fabric and then overcast edges to prevent stretching and raveling. Put 3⅜" darts in all four corners of each top and bottom piece, as shown in drawing 16-3. Duplicate the angle of this dart; it's important to the cushion's finished appearance.

Next, join the corresponding zipper strips with an appropriate

length of zipper. This creates a side band. Join that side band to the others to form a continuous loop. With fabric's right sides together, join the corresponding top and bottom pieces to the loop. Then press the seam open. To reinforce the seams, baste ¾" twill tape over them. Turn the fabric cover right side out and topstitch ⅛" on both sides of the seam through the twill tape.

Now stuff the cover with the muslin-covered stuffing.

Stuffing for back cushions is high-quality polyester batting. Seat cushions are stuffed with firm foam, cut 1" smaller in length and width and 2" thinner than cushion dimensions. Wrap them twice with polyester batting.

Lay the cushions in place on the platforms to complete your couch.

CHART OF SIZES FOR CUSHIONS

	Finished Cushion Sizes	Top & Bottom Panel Sizes (Cut 2)	Edge Band Sizes (Cut 1)	Zipper Strip Sizes (Cut 2)	Invisible Zipper Sizes (1)	Foam Sizes (1)
SEAT CUSHIONS	33" x 33"	39¾" x 39¾"	3¼" x 100"	2⅛" x 34"	34"	6" x 32" x 32"
	33" x 32"	39¾" x 38¾"	3¼" x 98"	2⅛" x 34"	34"	6" x 32" x 31"
	33" x 31"	39¾" x 37¾"	3¼" x 96"	2⅛" x 34"	34"	6" x 32" x 30"
	FOR SMALLER SIZES, FOLLOW SAME REGRESSION.					
BACK CUSHIONS	12½" x 24"	19¼" x 30¾"	3¼" x 61½"	2⅛" x 13½"	14"	No Foam
	12½" x 25"	19¼" x 31¾"	3¼" x 63½"	2⅛" x 13½"	14"	No Foam
	12½" x 26"	19¼" x 32¾"	3¼" x 65½"	2⅛" x 13½"	14"	No Foam
	FOR LARGER SIZES, FOLLOW SAME PROGRESSION.					

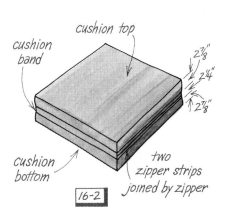

16-2

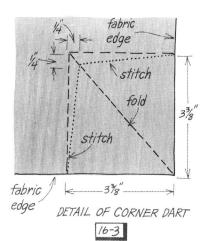

DETAIL OF CORNER DART

16-3

Oak Butcher Block Couch

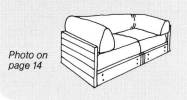

Photo on page 14

Oak butcher blocks, glued up by a cabinetmaker, form the sides and backs of this two-piece couch. You do the rest: add the oak base, put on the webbing that holds the cushions, and make the cushions. (If your shop is well equipped, of course, you can make the butcher blocks yourself.)

And you don't have to stop with what you see here. You can separate

...se two pieces like book ends
...dd another section between
...longate the couch.

...LL NEED: pencil ·
... square · handsaw · drill ·
¼" a... ...by 1¾" screw pilot ·
hamme... ...wrench · screwdriver ·
adjustab... ...ench · sandpaper and
finishing tools · sewing equipment and
sewing machine · serrated bread knife.
Helpful tools include a radial-arm saw,
table saw, or power circular saw; a drill
press; bar or pipe clamps; and an
electric carving knife.

MATERIALS LIST:

4 butcher blocks, red oak, 1¼" by 18½"
   by 37¼" (Have these glued up by a
   cabinetmaker.)
13' of 1¼" by 6" red oak
1 sheet of ¾" shop grade plywood
16 flathead screws, 1¾" by #8
32 Allen-head bolts, ¼" by 2", with nuts
32 washers, ¼", brass (or painted black)
32 washers, ¼", regular
66' of rubber upholstery webbing,
   2" wide
48 rubber webbing clamps, 2"
1-pound box of 3d box nails
White glue
2 blocks of soft foam, 4" thick by
   38" square
2 blocks of medium foam, 4" thick by
   38" square
1 foam block, 1' by 1' by 12'
Foam adhesive

13 yards of fabric, 45" wide
Matching polyester thread
13 yards of polyester batting
Danish oil

HERE'S HOW

Begin by cutting the 1¼" red oak to
size. You'll need two 36" lengths
and two 37¼" lengths. By buying
the hardwood already "dimensioned" (surfaced to the proper
width and thickness), you can
eliminate the need for a radial-arm
saw or table saw. (If you can't buy
the oak "dimensioned," have the
cabinetmaker who makes the
butcher blocks do this work.) When
cutting the pieces to length, use a
square to mark and check your cuts.

Next, cut eight 6" by 34¾" pieces
from the sheet of plywood. Glue
and screw these together with 1¾"
screws to form two squares (see
drawing 17-1). Stretch and fasten
rubber webbing across the top of
each square, spaced evenly as
shown in drawing 17-1. Fasten the
clamps with 3-penny box nails.

Join the oak pieces around each
plywood framework as shown in
drawing 17-1, counterboring a ⅞"
diameter hole about ½" deep, then
drilling ¼" bolt holes through both

the oak and the plywood. Be sure
that all oak pieces meet flush and
smoothly at the corners.

Then disassemble the oak, make
any necessary adjustments, and
sand. Round the edges slightly as
you sand. Wipe clean and apply two
coats of Danish oil.

Last, make the cushions. For each
seat, glue together one soft block
and one medium block of 38"-
square foam (soft goes up). Wrap
once around with polyester batting;
then make a knife-edge cover, as
explained on page 78. The cover
should be about 2" smaller than the
stuffing so it will fit tightly.

After slicing one corner off the 1'

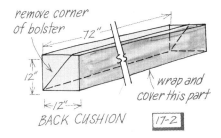

by 1' by 12' bolster for the back,
as shown in drawing 17-2, wrap it
once around with batting and cover
it the same way you covered the
cushions.

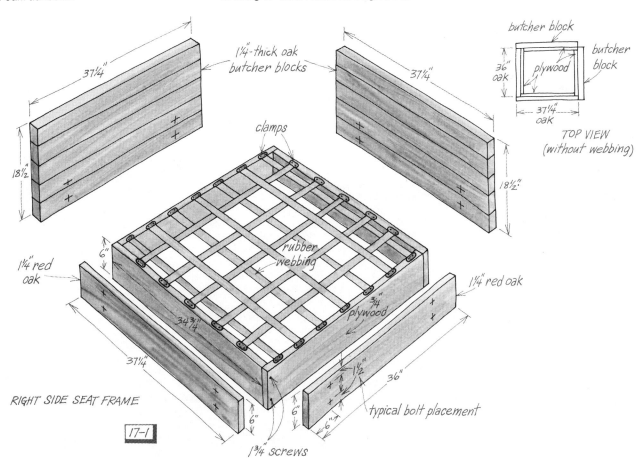

COFFEE TABLES

Three styles made from a variety of materials

Herringbone Coffee Table

Photo on facing page

Intricately laid oak in a herringbone pattern makes the surface of this large coffee table look as if it were created by a master craftsman. But you can duplicate this work in about half a day: it's surprisingly easy to make from oak flooring.

If this table is too large for your room, you can reduce it by increments of the flooring modules to whatever size you want. Or would you prefer an end table? Just make the top a small rectangle and lengthen the legs.

TOOLS YOU'LL NEED: pencil · measuring tape · square · radial-arm or table saw · drill · #10 by 1½" screw pilot · mastic spreader · bar or pipe clamps · screwdriver · sandpaper and finishing tools. *Helpful tools* include a router with a ⅜" quarter-round bit, and a power sander.

MATERIALS LIST:

16 sq. ft. of ⁵⁄₁₆" flooring
½ sheet (4' by 4') of ½" plywood
16' of ¾" by 3" oak
6' of ⁵⁄₄" by 8" oak
Wood flooring mastic
White glue
12 flathead screws, 1½" by #10
Detergent
Wood paste filler (natural or oak)
Clear polyurethane finish

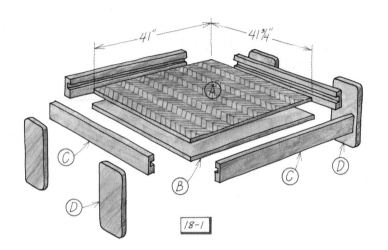

18-1

HERE'S HOW

First make the top from wood parquet flooring(A)glued to a plywood base(B). The ⁵⁄₁₆-inch-thick flooring comes in precut, prejoined blocks, normally about 1 square foot, with a paper backing.

Without using mastic, lay the blocks out on the plywood base, paper backing facing up. Arrange the wood grain and coloration for best appearance. Then pick the blocks up, remembering where they go.

Prepare a bowl of lukewarm water and detergent. Spread the mastic on the plywood thinly according to the label directions. Lay the blocks in place, paper side up, aligned with the plywood's straightest edge, tight fitting and in straight rows.

Dip a rag in the detergent water and scrub the backing off the tiles. As you do this, fit them all snugly together by hand. When you finish this process, lay a flat board on top, place a heavy object on the board,

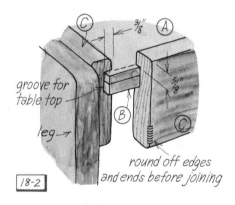

groove for table top

leg

round off edges and ends before joining

18-2

and let the mastic dry overnight.

The next day you can trim off the edges. To duplicate the table size shown, cut the top to 41" by 41¾". Be sure that all corners are true 90°.

Fill all the gaps and cracks, using a wood paste filler (available at the flooring dealer). Sand off the excess by hand. Then you can either belt-sand the top until flat and smooth or, for a minimal charge, take it to a planing mill or large lumberyard and have it run through a drum sander.

Next, cut the groove in the ¾" by

Herringbone Coffee Table *See facing page. Design: Don Vandervort*

3" frame pieces (C) according to drawing 18-2, using a router or table saw.

Round the four outer edges of these pieces, using a router and ⅜" quarter-round bit or using sandpaper. Then get the exact length for these pieces by measuring the top. If your top is exactly the same size as the one shown, two of these pieces will be 40¼" and the other two 41". Cut them to length and round off their top edges and ends, as shown in drawing 18-2.

Be sure the frame pieces fit properly around the top; then glue and clamp them with two bar or pipe clamps going each direction. Wipe off excess glue.

Cut the legs (D) to 16" and round all edges. Use a square to mark and check your cuts.

When the glue is dry, remove the clamps and turn the framed top upside down on a flat surface. Glue, clamp, and screw each leg in place, flush with the table's top edge and side.

Fill and sand; apply two coats of penetrating polyurethane finish.

Pine Parsons Table

Photo on page 20

Made from inexpensive #3 Common pine, this small table gains its distinction from the wood's knots, streaks, and stains. And you can make it practically any size, from long and low to the somewhat tall, square shape shown. The following directions are for making the table shown. To alter the shape, just modify the materials list according to the dimensions you wish.

TOOLS YOU'LL NEED: pencil · measuring tape · square · handsaw · radial-arm or table saw · drill · ½" and 1" bits · hammer · nailset (or large nail) · Allen wrench (or adjustable wrench) · sandpaper and finishing tools. *Helpful*

tools include pipe or bar clamps and an electric sander.

MATERIALS LIST:

63' of 1 by 4 pine, #3 Common
10' of 1 by 2
½ sheet of ¾" particle board
8 Allen-head bolts (or hex-head bolts), ⅜" by 1", with washers and T-nuts
1-pound box of 3d finishing nails
1-pound box of 5d finishing nails
White glue
Wood filler
Clear polyurethane finish

HERE'S HOW

Remember that the materials list, the drawings, and these instructions are for making a table the same size as that pictured on page 20. If you wish to alter the size, or if the pine you buy is not *exactly* ¾" by 3½", you must figure the necessary changes into the plans.

Begin by cutting to size all of the following pieces except (G) and (H). Use a square to mark and check your cuts. (For more about cutting, see page 67.)

(Continued on page 20)

Pine Parsons Table *Design: Greg Smith, The Just Plain Smith Co.*

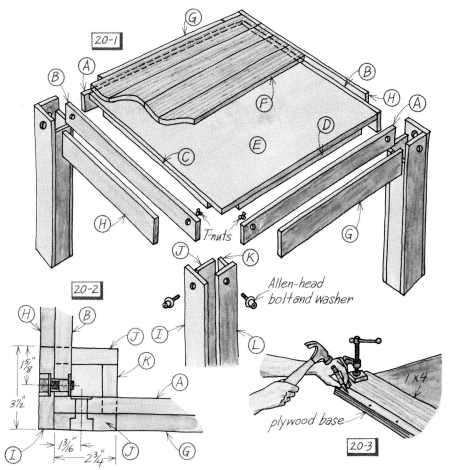

. . . Continued from page 19

(A) Two 1 by 4s (ripped to 2¾"
wide), 28"

(B) Two 1 by 4s (ripped to 2?
wide), 26½"

(C and D) Four 1 by 2s, 22½"

(E) One piece of ¾" particle
board, 26½" by 26½"

(F) Eight 1 by 4s, 28"

(I) Four 1 by 4s, 21½"

(J) Four 1 by 4s (ripped to 2¾"
wide), 18"

(K) Four 1 by 4s (ripped to 2"
wide), 18"

(L) Four 1 by 4s (ripped to 2¾"
wide), 21½"

First glue and nail with 3-penny
nails the 1 by 2 cleats, (C) and (D),
on all four edges of the particle
board. Keep them flush with the
particle board edges.

Mark and drill holes in pieces (A)
and (B) for T-nuts, according to
drawing 20-2. Then glue and nail
with 5d nails the (A) and (B) pieces
to (C) and (D), respectively. Keep
the top edges of (A) and (B) flush
with the board's top surface.

Counterbore and drill the bolt
holes in (I), referring to drawing
20-2; then glue and nail together
the legs. Keep all pieces flush and
square with each other.

Now cover the table top with the
(F) pieces. Begin by spreading glue
on the underside of one piece and
laying it flush along the outer edges
of (A). If you have clamps, clamp
down the 1 by 4, protecting the pine
by adding a scrap wood block
beneath the clamp's jaws. Blind nail
the 1 by 4 to the particle board
with 5-penny finishing nails, as
shown in drawing 20-3.

Spread glue on the bottom and
the adjoining edge of the next 1 by
4 (F), and butt the glued edge
against the fastened piece. Before
nailing, use bar clamps (if you have
them) to cinch the new piece tightly
against the first one. Blind nail as
before. Continue this process for
succeeding 1 by 4s across the rest
of the surface. Wipe off excess glue.

Next, bolt the legs in place
according to drawing 20-2. Measure
the distance between them for an
accurate fit of the (G) and (H)
pieces. Cut those pieces to length.
Glue and nail them in place with
3-penny finishing nails, nailing
primarily from (A) and (B) into (G)
and (H), respectively.

Set and fill all exposed nails; then
sand. If necessary, refill the holes
and sand again. Wipe away all
sawdust and apply two coats of
polyurethane finish.

Glass-Top Table

Combining cherry hardwood and a square slab of smoked glass, this simple coffee table takes advantage of two inherently beautiful materials.

Is it difficult to make? Not at all. You just cut and drill the wood pieces and dowel them together, then set the glass on top.

TOOLS YOU'LL NEED: pencil · measuring tape · square · handsaw · chisel · C-clamps · hammer or mallet · sandpaper and finishing tools. *Helpful tools* include a radial-arm or table saw, dado blade, drill or drill press with a ¾" bit, and power sander.

MATERIALS LIST:
16' of 1½" by 5½" cherry (or equivalent)
About 7' of ¾" doweling (optional)
Smoked glass top, ½" thick by 32" square
White glue
Wood filler
Danish oil

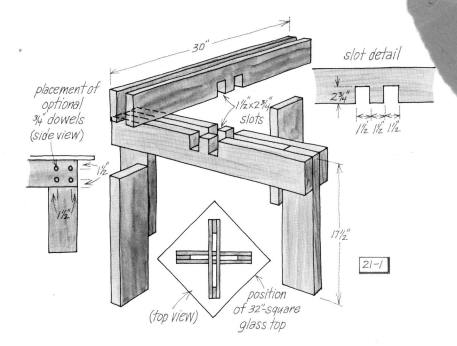

placement of optional ¾" dowels (side view)

1½" 1½"

30"

1½"x2¾" slots

slot detail

2¾"

1½" 1½" 1½"

17½"

21-1

(top view)

position of 32"-square glass top

HERE'S HOW

Begin by cutting all the wood to length. You'll need four pieces 17½" long and four pieces 30" long. Mark and check all cuts with a square.

Next mark with a square and cut the slots in the longer crosspieces as specified in drawing 21-1 (for more about cutting slots, see page 69). Sand or file the slots smooth. Cut the slots carefully; if they are too long or short, the base won't fit together properly. Slide the pieces together to check for fit.

Now assemble the base in two pieces, each with two legs and two crosspieces. Glue and sandwich a leg between two crosspieces, checking with a square for the proper 90° angle and making sure that the ends are flush before clamping the pieces together. Protect the wood from the jaws of the clamps by slipping scraps between the jaws and the wood. Repeat this joinery process for the other three leg-and-crosspiece joints.

Slide together the two halves to form the complete base. Let the glue dry; then remove the clamps. Now, if you wish, you can drill ¾" holes and add decorative ¾" dowels at each joint. (For more about drilling, see page 70.) These dowels are not necessary structurally if the glue joints are properly made. You can either drill the holes all the way through the pieces and pound the dowels through, or you can drill short "dummy" holes and insert short dowel pieces. Cut off excess doweling and sand the ends flush.

Now sand the entire base, slightly rounding all edges. Fill any holes or defects and sand again. Repeat if necessary. Apply two coats of Danish oil and allow to dry.

To complete the table, simply set the glass top (purchased and cut at a glass dealer's) on the base. You can position the top either parallel or diagonal to the base's cross-pieces. If you don't want to set the glass directly on the wood, add a small, black rubber tack to each corner of the base.

Glass-Top Table   *Design: Don Vandervort*

Particle Board Chair

Handy pouch in backrest stores magazines.
See facing page.
Design: Lisa Scott

Cantilever Chair

See page 24.
Design: Laurence S. Mayers

CHAIRS

. . . designed for comfort, beauty, practicality

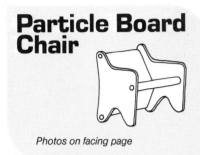

Particle Board Chair

Photos on facing page

Combining handsome, low-cost seating and a novel magazine holder, this particle board and canvas chair is easy enough that you can make it in one day.

One sheet of particle board forms the two chair sides; the sling is sewn from canvas and looped around three dowels; and the dowels bolt to the sides.

TOOLS YOU'LL NEED: pencil · measuring tape · straightedge · compass · saber saw · half-round file · drill · ¼", ⅝", and 1⅜" bits · screwdriver · tweezers · sandpaper and finishing tools · sewing equipment and sewing machine · serrated bread knife. *A helpful tool* is a hole saw.

MATERIALS LIST:

1 sheet of ¾" particle board
7' of 1⅜" doweling (closet-pole rounds)
6 slot-head bolts, ¼" by 2½", with washers and nuts
6 black plastic caps, 2"-diameter lip (optional)
Clear polyurethane finish
2 yards of chair canvas, 29" wide
Matching polyester thread
2 foam rolls, 2" diameter by 24" (¾" refrigeration insulation tubing or race-car roll-bar padding also works well)
Foam adhesive or adhesive tape

HERE'S HOW

Begin by transferring the pattern shown in drawing 23-1 onto a piece of particle board. Use a saber saw to cut out the shape, file and sand any rough edges or irregular cuts, and then lay that piece on the uncut portion of the particle board as a pattern for marking the second chair side. Mark the second side and cut it out. File and sand any irregularities, wipe clean, and apply a polyurethane finish.

Next, mark and drill the ¼" holes through the two sides where indicated in drawing 23-1. Cut three pieces from the closet pole rounds. Mark and drill first the ⅝" hole, then the ¼" hole, in both ends of each 1⅜" round as shown in drawing 23-2. Be sure that the holes intersect on center.

Wrap two of these dowels with foam. If you use a foam roll, cut it in half lengthwise with the bread knife. Cut a V-shaped trough along

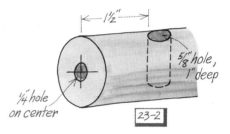

each square = 3"   23-1

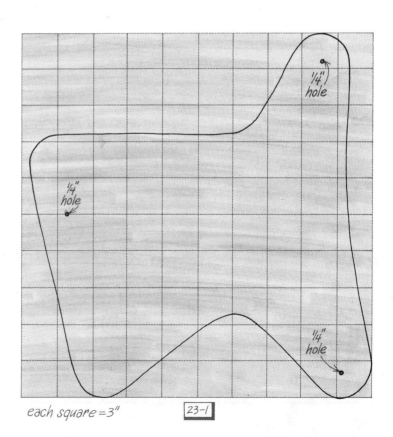

the center of each half and glue it back together around the dowel. (For fastening other types of padding around the dowels, try adhesive tape.)

When you put the padding around the dowel, either hold it back from the ⅝" hole or cut a hole through it so you can push a nut into the ⅝" hole during assembly.

Sew the sling as shown in drawing 24-1. (For more about sling sewing techniques, see page 76.)

The magazine pouch is simply a rectangular fabric scrap that's stitched to the back.

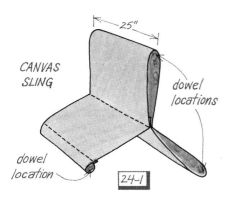

For a finishing touch, you can cover the bolt heads by cutting a round groove around each one and inserting a black plastic cap, as shown in drawing 24-2.

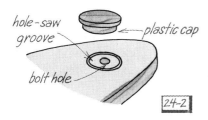

Now fasten all three dowels to one side, using a bolt and nut for each one as shown in drawing 24-3. Hold the nut in place with a pair of tweezers. Slide the sling onto the dowels (see drawing 24-1) and attach the other side panel, using the other three nuts and bolts.

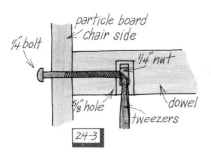

Cantilever Chair

Photo on page 22

Elegant yet simple, this cantilevered birch chair has a trestle base that's glued and screwed together. The simple knife-edge cushions are supported by a canvas sling that stretches from the chair's back rail to its front rail.

Though the primary base components on the chair pictured on page 22 were cut from a special, multi-laminated Finnish plywood, we recommend that for the sake of cost and availability you work with standard birch or a similar hardwood.

TOOLS YOU'LL NEED: pencil · measuring tape · square · protractor · handsaw · file · drill · #10 by 1¼" and #12 by 3" pilot bits and ⅜" plug cutter · C-clamps · screwdriver · sandpaper and finishing tools · sewing equipment · sewing machine. *Helpful tools* include a radial-arm or table saw, a power sander, and pipe or bar clamps.

MATERIALS LIST:

15' of ¾" by 3½" birch
10' of 1¾" by 1¾" birch
¼ sheet of ¼" A-D plywood
12 flathead screws, 1¼" by #10
14 pan-head screws, 1¼" by #10, with washers
8 flathead screws, 3" by #12
White glue
Wood filler
Danish oil, boiled linseed oil, turpentine, and satin polyurethane finish
1⅓ yards of chair canvas, 30" wide
5 pounds of shredded foam
3⅓ yards of upholstery fabric, 36" wide
Matching polyester thread
6 buttons, ¾"
6 upholstery buttons

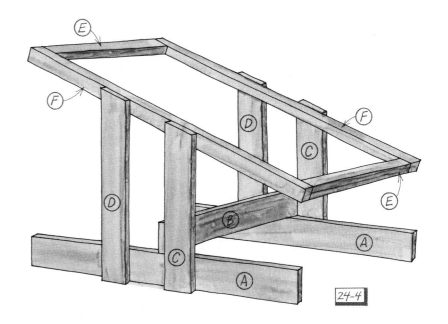

HERE'S HOW

Begin by cutting the pieces to size. You won't need a radial-arm or table saw if your dealer sells "dimensioned" hardwood (surfaced to the proper thicknesses and widths). Otherwise, you might take the wood to a cabinetmaker to have it dimensioned. If you do the cutting yourself, be sure to use a square to mark and check all cuts. Use the following schedule.

- (A) Two ¾" by 3½" pieces, 33"
- (B) One ¾" by 3½" piece, 29"
- (C) Two ¾" by 3½" pieces, 17"
- (D) Two ¾" by 3½" pieces, 21"
- (E) Two 1¾" by 1¾" pieces, 24"
- (F) Two 1¾" by 1¾" pieces, 35½"

In addition, cut the plywood to 20½" by 21¾". You'll also need two plywood scraps, each 1½" by 20½", for fastening the canvas to the frame. And make an additional cut at one end of the (C) and (D) pieces: cut each one off at a 65° angle, marking the cut first with a protractor and square.

Mark placements of the (C) pieces on the (A) pieces, then glue and clamp them in place. (Put scraps beneath the jaws of the clamps to keep them from denting the wood.) Use a square to make sure the pieces are exactly perpendicular.

While the glue dries, make the frame from pieces (E) and (F). Working on a flat surface, glue and screw together these pieces, counterboring the 3" screws for decorative wood plugs. Round off the corners with a file or sander.

Attach (B) to both (C) pieces, using glue and 1¼" flathead screws, counterbored for wood plugs. Once piece (B) is in place, add (D) the same way you attached (C) to (A).

Next, join the seat frame—pieces (E) and (F)—to the uprights, (C) and (D). Glue the pieces and clamp them together. You can counterbore pilot holes and screw the pieces together either now or after the glue dries.

Either cut short dowel lengths or cut plugs from hardwood scraps

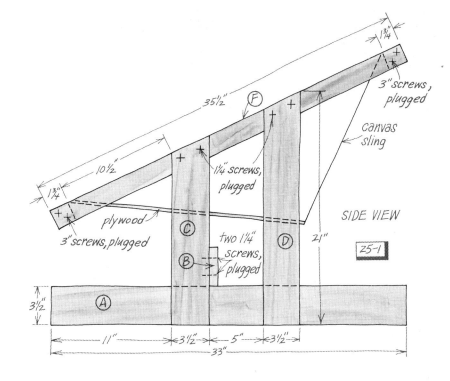

with a plug cutter to fill all counterbored screw holes. Glue the plugs or dowels in place and sand them flush.

Sand all surfaces, rounding the edges slightly. To duplicate the finish on the chair pictured on page 22, sand with 120-grit sandpaper until smooth. Then apply and reapply Danish oil, wet sanding it into the wood with 220-grit wet-and-dry abrasive paper after each coat. Next, mix equal parts boiled linseed oil, satin polyurethane varnish, and turpentine. Brush this mixture onto the wood and wet sand it with 400-grit paper. Repeat applications until you have the finish you wish.

Cut and hem the 43" by 20½" sling. Attach both ends to the frame

as shown in drawing 25-2. Both cushions are simply 4"-thick knife-edge cushions. The back is 23" by 26"; the seat is 27" by 26". Attach upholstery buttons as shown in drawing 25-3.

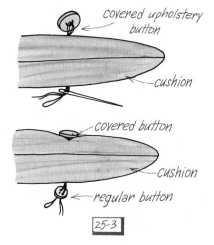

ADJUSTABLE FURNITURE

These two pieces flip-flop for many uses

Folding Three-level Table

Photos on pages 27 and 28

It folds flat, stands as a dining table, shortens to an intermediate height, and compresses to a coffee table; this multilevel portable table can fill dozens of needs. Depending upon how you set the top on its base, the table's height adjusts to 16, 24, or 28 inches. And by separating the base from the top, you can flatten the table for transporting.

This table can be made in less than a day, and because it's built from softwood (vertical grain fir), it's relatively inexpensive.

TOOLS YOU'LL NEED: pencil · measuring tape · square · handsaw · drill · ¼", 1", and 1¼" bits · #8 by 1¼" and #8 by 2" screw pilots · screwdriver · sandpaper and finishing tools. *Helpful tools* include a radial-arm or table saw, drill press, and power sander.

MATERIALS LIST:
6' of 2 by 2 Clear fir
5' of 1 by 3 Clear fir
22' of 1 by 6 Clear fir
10' of 1¼"-diameter rounds
9' of 1"-diameter rounds
24 flathead screws, 1¼" by #8
20 flathead screws, 2" by #8
2 slot-head bolts, ¼" by 3", with nuts
4 washers, ¼"
Waterproof glue
Wood filler
Clear polyurethane finish

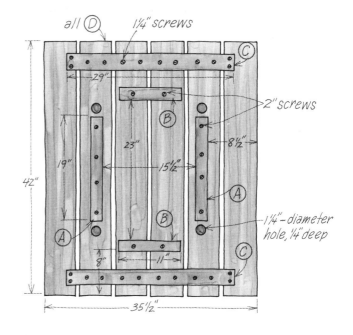

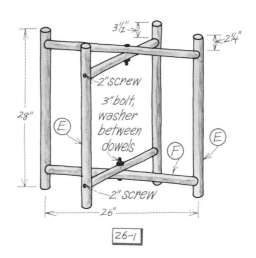

26-1

Folding Table *Adjust table to three heights. For third position, see page 28.*

HERE'S HOW

Begin by cutting the various pieces to length according to the following cutting schedule. Use a square to mark and check your cuts.

(A) Two 2 by 2s, 19"
(B) Two 2 by 2s, 11"
(C) Two 1 by 3s, 29"
(D) Six 1 by 6s, 42"
(E) Four 1¼"-diameter rounds, 28"
(F) Four 1"-diameter rounds, 26"

On a flat surface, lay out the 1 by 6s (D) for the top, spaced ½" apart as shown in drawing 26-1. Glue the 1 by 3s (C) to them as shown in that same drawing, drilling pilot holes and driving two 1¼" screws into each 1 by 6.

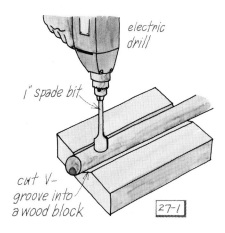

electric drill

1" spade bit

cut V-groove into a wood block

27-1

Add the 2 by 2s (A and B), gluing, drilling pilot holes, and driving 2" screws.

To make the base, drill 1"-diameter holes, ¼" deep, located where shown in drawing 26-1. For drilling, cradle each round in a jig like the one shown in drawing 27-1. Be sure that both holes in each round are aligned exactly parallel with each other. Apply glue and push the 1" rounds (F) into the holes in the 1¼" rounds (E). Then drill pilot holes through (E) into the end of (F) and fasten with 2" screws.

When the glue dries, interlock the base's two halves and drill ¼" holes for the slot-head bolts at the midpoint of the 1" rounds (F). Poke

Folding table at intermediate height. See page 26.

the bolts through, placing a washer between the rounds, and add final washers and nuts.

With the table top's underside facing up, place base on it, on end so that the ends of (E) are at the approximate locations specified in drawing 26-1. Mark the exact locations and drill the 1¼"-diameter holes, ¼" deep.

Sand all parts, fill any defects, resand, and apply a clear polyurethane finish.

Multiposition Tube Seat

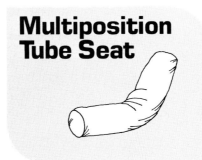

Flop it, fold it, plump it, squash it, coil it: this tube becomes any kind of seat or lounge you want it to be. Durable and lightweight, the tube is easy to sew from 14 feet of fabric; it's stuffed with styrofoam packing chips. (You can substitute styrene foam pellets; to find them, see "Plastics—Rods, Tubes, Sheets, Etc., Supply Centers" in the Yellow Pages.)

Though the tube shown in the photo was covered with vinyl for washability and durability, practically any heavy fabric is suitable.

TOOLS YOU'LL NEED: tape measure · sewing equipment · sewing machine

MATERIALS LIST:

4⅔ yards of fabric, 54" wide
Matching polyester thread
14" zipper
12 cubic feet of styrofoam chips or pellets

Multiposition Tube Seat

Design: Gordon C. Smith

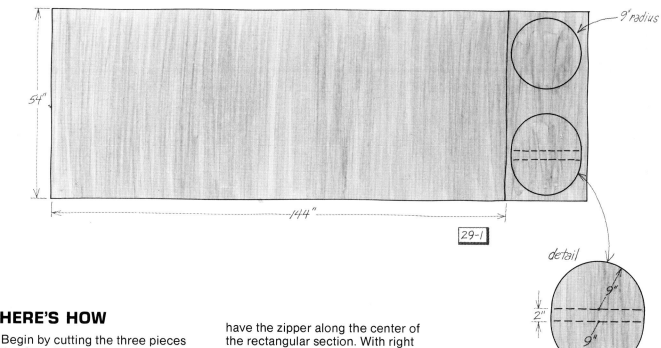

54"

144"

29-1

9" radius

detail

2"

9"

9"

HERE'S HOW

Begin by cutting the three pieces that form the tube from the yardage as shown in drawing 29-1. The two rounded pieces become the ends of the tube.

Fold the long piece of fabric in half along its length, with right sides facing together. Double-stitch the long edges together, allowing 1" for the seam. You now have a 12'-long tube with open ends.

As you can see in the plan, one end is to have a zipper and the other isn't. Cut the end that is to

have the zipper along the center of the rectangular section. With right sides together, stitch a 1" seam along the straight edge, using a basting or long stitch. Then insert the zipper according to package instructions. Double-stitch along the seam line on both sides of the zipper with a regular stitch. Finally, remove the basting stitches to reveal the zipper.

Open the zipper and, with right sides together, double-stitch the end pieces in place at each end of the tube, allowing 1" all around for

seams. Don't forget to leave the zipper open so you can turn the tube right side out.

Turn the tube right side out and fill it as full as seems right for your needs. The fuller it is, of course, the less flexible it will be. Zip it up and enjoy.

See more about working with fabrics on page 76.

Trestle Desk

*See facing page.
Design: Ivo Greghov,
Ibsen Nelson & Associates*

Redwood Plywood Desk   *See page 32. Design: Norman A. Plate*

*Desk top raises and lowers like a
drawing table; detail of drawer front
shows beauty of plywood edges.*

DESKS

One is simple, the other is more challenging

Trestle Desk

Photo on facing page

Where better to find a well-designed desk than in an architect's office where skilled designers need practical work surfaces? That's where this one was discovered. Its traits include simple construction, clean lines, and low cost. And though it makes a great desk, it can double as a good-looking, comfortable dining table.

The trestle base consists of three basic wood parts, and the top is a hollow-core door without a predrilled door knob hole. And the fact that all the joints are made with bolts means that it's as easy to disassemble for moving as it is to build.

The dimensions for lumber given in the materials list are standard softwood dimensions, but you can make the base from hardwood. In fact, the desk shown in the photo on page 30 has an oak base. When ordering a hardwood, remember that a 2 by 2 really measures 1½" by 1½" and a 2 by 8 is actually 1½" by 7½".

TOOLS YOU'LL NEED: pencil · measuring tape · square · handsaw · drill · ⁵⁄₁₆" bit · adjustable wrench · pliers · sandpaper and finishing tools. *Helpful tools* include a radial-arm or table saw, drill press, and socket set.

MATERIALS LIST:
Hollow-core birch door, 3' by 6'8", no knob hole
17' of Clear 2 by 2
17' of Clear 2 by 8
24 hex-head bolts, ¼" by 5"
24 acorn nuts, ¼"
48 washers, ¼"
Danish oil or clear polyurethane finish

HERE'S HOW

Begin by cutting all the pieces to the following lengths. Use a square to mark and check your cuts.
(A) Eight 2 by 2s, 24½" long
(B) Four 2 by 8s, 30" long
(C) One 2 by 8, 80" long
Next use the pencil, square, and measuring tape to mark hole

placements where specified in drawing 31-1.

Drill the holes through the various pieces (see page 70 for information about drilling straight, clean holes). Work precisely; all holes must line up to receive the bolts.

Though you can apply the finish either before or after assembly, sanding is best done before assembly. Sand everything except the door—it shouldn't need it.

Bolt together the base; if you didn't apply the finish before assembly, do that now. When the finish is dry, just set the door onto the base. Because the door isn't attached, you can turn it over and use the underside if the top gets marred.

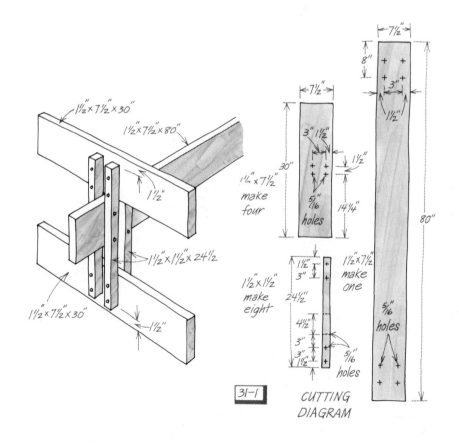

CUTTING DIAGRAM

Redwood Plywood Desk

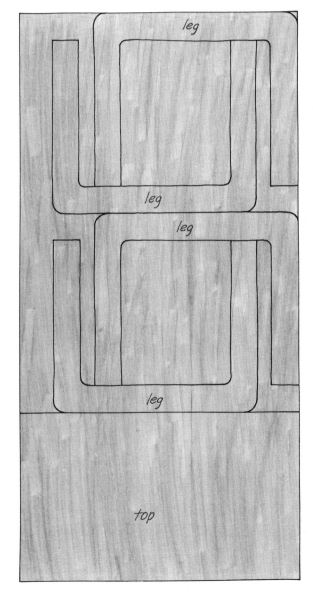

Photos on page 30

Work on it flat or tilt up the back and use it like a drawing board: this desk has an adjustable top. Transforming plywood edges into handsome visual detailing, this desk makes elegant use of a rustic material—plywood house siding. Of course, you can't buy plywood as thick as the legs of the desk—they consist of four thicknesses of 5⁄8" plywood, glued together. The top is made from two thicknesses, glued together and covered by a sheet of glass.

Two large drawers glide freely beneath the top, offering plenty of handy storage.

This desk is one of the more difficult projects in this book. Having the right tools can make a world of difference. Because of the large amount of sanding required, a belt sander is a must. And a radial-arm or table saw is important for cutting the drawer pieces. More about tools follows.

TOOLS YOU'LL NEED: pencil · measuring tape · square · compass · saber saw · radial-arm or table saw · drill · 1⁄16" and 3⁄8" bits, expansive bit · short bar or pipe clamps or 7" C-clamps · hammer · nailset (or large nail) · screwdriver · belt sander · sandpaper and finishing tools.

MATERIALS LIST:

2 sheets of 5⁄8" Premium rough-sawn redwood siding
4 hardwood dowels, 1 5⁄16" by 5'*
1 pair of 22"-long under-counter drawer glides*
1 pair of 22"-long side-mounting drawer glides
2 casement window locking guides, 12"
2 pipe straps, 1 1⁄2"
4 round-head screws, 1" by #8
1-pound box of 4d finishing nails
4 leg levelers

---

*If these materials are not available at your lumberyard or builder's supply, ask your dealer to order them specially for you.

1 sheet of glass, 1⁄4" by 47 3⁄8" by 29 3⁄4", edges finished
4 plastic tabs for holding glass, 1⁄8" by 1" by 1"
White glue
Wood filler (redwood)
Clear polyurethane finish

HERE'S HOW

Begin by laying out the pieces on the plywood sheets as shown in drawing 32-1. Refer to drawings 33-1 and 33-3 for exact dimensions.

The pair of legs at each side of the desk is made up of four plywood thicknesses glued together. As you cut these pieces from the plywood sheets, be sure that, when they are laid one on top of another, their contours will match precisely. In other words, mark and cut them all exactly the same.

Cutting is the next step. Use the saber saw (for helpful information on cutting, see page 67). Also cut out the two pieces for the desk top. Be sure to cut to the *outside* of your lines.

Now glue together the pieces: four for each pair of legs and two for the top. Clamp the legs as shown in drawing 33-2. (Be sure not to glue up more at one time than you have clamps for.) Instead of clamping together the pieces for the top, you can lay them on a flat surface and put something heavy on them. Before letting the glue dry, make sure that all edges are flush and wipe away excess glue.

To make the drawer fronts, you'll need to cut twenty-two 1" by 12"

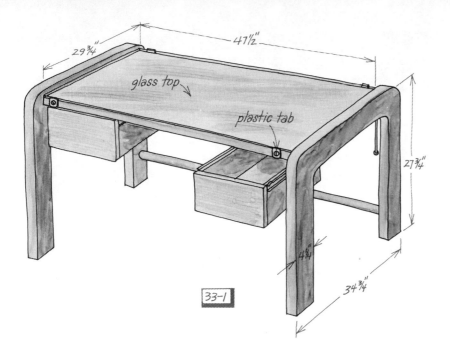

33-1

glass top
plastic tab
29¾"
47½"
27¾"
34¾"
4¼"

evenly on a flat surface; then let the glue dry.

While the glue dries, assemble the drawers from plywood scraps as shown in drawing 33-4. Glue and

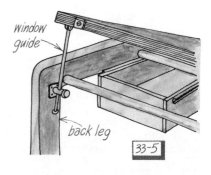

10⅝"
20¾"
back 5¾"
side
6"
10⅝"
front plate 5¾"
6"
side
eleven 1"-wide strips of ⅝" plywood
bottom
11⅞"
20¾"
front
10⅝"
33-4

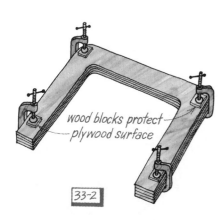

wood blocks protect plywood surface

33-2

pieces from the ⅝" plywood scraps. Glue them and clamp them together in two sets of 11 strips each, edges facing out and flush at both ends and surfaces. Wipe off excess glue. When the glue dries, trim ¹⁄₁₆" off both ends to make them perfectly straight.

Now fill all gaps and crevices in the plywood edges and prepare to sand. The object is to sand all plywood *edges* perfectly smooth and flat. Do not sand the rough-sawn plywood faces. The sanding will take a degree of patience and care. Start with coarse sandpaper on the belt sander and work to a fine paper, refilling gaps if necessary. Finish with a fine, careful hand sanding. Sand the inside curves of the legs by hand too.

Now it's time to drill the holes for the 1⁵⁄₁₆"-diameter dowels. Set the expansion bit for a 1⁵⁄₁₆" hole and drill a test hole through a piece of scrap. Force the end of each dowel into the hole to be sure that the fit is snug but not so tight you won't be able to get the dowel into it. Drill 1½"-deep holes, placed where shown in drawing 33-3. If

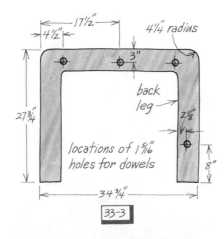

17½"
4½"
4¼ radius
3"
back leg
27¾"
2⅛"
locations of 1⁵⁄₁₆ holes for dowels
8"
34¾"
33-3

necessary, adjust the bit's diameter slightly for each dowel. Be sure to drill straight (for more about drilling, see page 70).

Cut the four dowels to 50⅜". After squirting a little glue into the dowel holes, pound all four dowels into one pair of legs first. Then pound the other pair of legs onto the dowels, protecting the wood by holding a scrap wood block against the legs as you pound. Wipe off excess glue.

Make sure all four legs stand

nail the joints with 4-penny finishing nails.

When the glue on the desk base is dry, set the top in place without the glass. Fasten the top to the dowel at the desk's front, screwing one pipe clamp to the underside at each end; use 1" screws.

Fasten the back of the desk top to the back legs, as shown in drawing 33-5, using window guides.

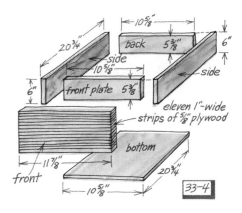

window guide
back leg
33-5

Drill ⅜" holes and install leg levelers on undersides of all four legs, following instructions on the levelers' package. Also install drawer glides, following the instructions on their packages. (Split up the two pairs: use one side glide and one top guide for each drawer.) The top-mounted glides screw onto the dowels.

Give all edges a final sanding and apply two coats of clear polyurethane finish.

Set the glass in place. Screw a small square of plastic to each corner at the front and back of the top to hold the glass in place when you raise and lower the top.

DINING TABLES

Two butcher-block styles: one round, one rectangular

Round Pedestal Table

Photo on facing page

For making most butcher block table tops, you need a variety of somewhat sophisticated tools: a jointer, a doweling jig, and long clamps. Not so with this butcher block style table—all you need is glue, a hammer, and nails.

And the wood pedestal is even easier to make than the top. It's just a paper drum covered with 1 by 2s.

Combined, the base and top make an inexpensive, handsome table with ample knee and elbow space for eight persons.

TOOLS YOU'LL NEED: pencil · measuring tape · square · yardstick · saber saw · handsaw · chisel · plane · drill · 5/32" bit · hammer · nailset · screwdriver · sandpaper and finishing tools. *Helpful tools* include a radial-arm or table saw, or a jointer, and a power sander.

MATERIALS LIST:
144' of Clear 2 by 2
94' of Clear 1 by 2
¼ sheet of ¾" A-D plywood
6 round-head screws, 1½" by #10
28-gallon paper drum
1-pound box ¾" carpet tacks
5-pound box 8d finishing nails
Resin glue
Danish oil or polyurethane finish

HERE'S HOW

Begin by cutting the lumber to length. Use a square to mark and check your cuts. Here's what you'll need:

- (A) Six 2 by 2s, 4'
- (B) Six 2 by 2s, 5'
- (C) Fifteen 2 by 2s, 6'
- (D) One 2 by 2, 54"
- (E) Forty 1 by 2s, 28"

Softwood boards have rounded edges. Before joining the 2 by 2s that form the top, you must remove those rounded edges that will face upward. To do this, run them through a table saw, radial-arm saw, or jointer, have them ripped at the lumberyard, or take them to a cabinetmaker or planing mill.

If you have a table saw, save money and time by buying half as many 2 by 4s instead of the 2 by 2s, ripping them in half, and facing the ripped edge of each half upward for the table's top surface.

Next lay the 2 by 2s upside down

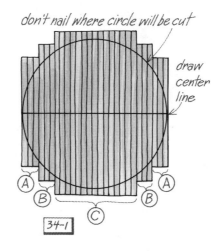

don't nail where circle will be cut

draw center line

34-1

on a flat surface as shown in drawing 34-1. To help keep them centered with each other during assembly, draw a line across the center of each, using a tape measure and square. Then align these marks as you work.

Starting at the middle, glue two 2 by 2s to each other and nail them every 8", using 8-penny finishing nails as shown in drawing 34-2. Don't nail where you'll be cutting the circular top.

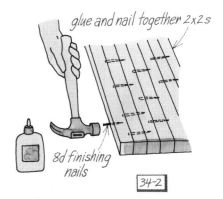

glue and nail together 2x2s

8d finishing nails

34-2

Work progressively outward from this middle pair, gluing and nailing through the edges that will be hidden. Keep all pieces flat, and wipe away excess glue. When you get to the two outside 2 by 2s, set the nail heads below the surface and fill the holes.

To cut out the circular top, start by tacking one end of a yardstick to the table top's center and, holding a pencil at the 33-inch mark, turn the yardstick like a large clock hand. Then use a saber saw to cut along this line.

To make the base, stand the paper drum right side up. Measure 28" up from the floor and draw a

Round Pedestal Table *See facing page. Design: Rick Morrall*

drum, and hold it in place by driving carpet tacks (four per slat) from the inside.

When roughly half the drum is covered by 1 by 2s, place the others loosely around the unfinished part to determine whether they must be planed or sawn to fit. This way, you can trim a little from each instead of a lot from only one.

Mark the drum's inside diameter on the ¾" plywood and cut it, using a saber saw. Center the plywood circle on the underside of the table top and attach it with glue and six 1½" screws. Then brace the top by nailing and gluing a 2 by 2 crosspiece on the underside (see drawing 35-3).

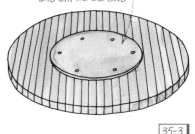

attach plywood with glue and six 1½" screws

35-3

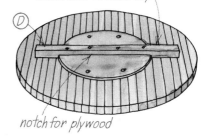

add 2 x 2 for support on underside of table top

notch for plywood

glue and tack slats to paper barrel

notched slat

35-1   Ⓔ

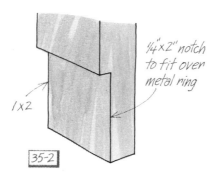

¼"x 2" notch to fit over metal ring

1 x 2

35-2

line around the drum at this level. Cut the drum along this line, using the saber saw.

Notch each of the 1 by 2s with a saw and chisel about ¼" by 2" to fit over the metal ring at the drum's bottom. Then glue each 1 by 2 liberally where it will contact the

notch top of barrel to fit 2 x 2 brace

Sand the top until flat and smooth, and lightly sand the 1 by 2s around the base. Apply two or three coats of Danish oil or polyurethane finish.

Butcher Block Parsons Table

This table looks as if it's made from 2 by 4s glued together to form a large slab, but it isn't. The top is actually made from 1 by 2s milled at the lumberyard to remove their rounded edges and glued and screwed to a plywood base. This easier, faster process saves immensely on the cost of lumber. The technique also trims the table's weight and your wait for the finished table.

TOOLS YOU'LL NEED: pencil · measuring tape · square · handsaw · chisel · drill · ½" bit, #8 by 1" and #9 by 2" screw pilots, and plug cutter · bar or pipe clamps · hammer · screwdriver · sandpaper and finishing tools. *Helpful tools* include a radial-arm or table saw, jointer, drill press, and power sander.

MATERIALS LIST:

200' of 1 by 2 Clear fir, edges milled
21' of 2 by 4 Clear fir, edges milled
21' of 2 by 4 Common fir
11' of 4 by 4 Clear fir
1 sheet of ¾" A-D plywood
6' of ½" hardwood doweling
2 boxes (200) flathead screws, 1" by #8
36 flathead screws, 2" by #9
1-pound box of 3d finishing nails
White glue
Wood filler
Danish oil or clear polyurethane finish

HERE'S HOW

Rather than cutting all 1 by 2s to exact length at first, cut them slightly long—to 7'—and trim them after assembly. If possible, have the ¾" plywood cut to 81" by 38¼" at the lumberyard (38¼" is slightly undersize, in case the lumberyard's ripping of the 1 by 2 edges removes more than planned).

Starting at the midpoint of each 1 by 2, mark each for screw placement as shown in drawing 36-1. Coat the underside of one 1 by 2 liberally with glue; drill 1" screw pilot holes, countersunk ¼";

Butcher Block Parsons Table   *Design: Peter O. Whiteley*

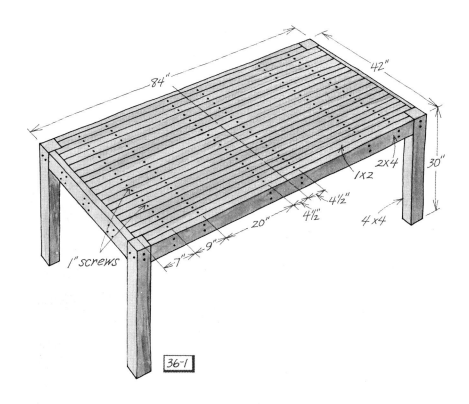

and screw the 1 by 2 to the plywood base. The 1 by 2 should overhang the base's edge by about ½" throughout its length.

Repeat with a second 1 by 2: glue its edges as well as its underside, and then align the screw holes and clamp it against the first 1 by 2 with a bar or pipe clamp before screwing it down (see drawing 37-1). Wipe off excess glue. Continue the process for the remaining 1 by 2s.

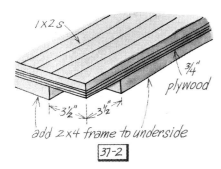

draw 2x2s tight before screwing them down

37-1

of Clear 2 by 4s, on edge, around the sides and ends of the table top. Attach it with screws as detailed in drawing 37-3 and plug the screw holes.

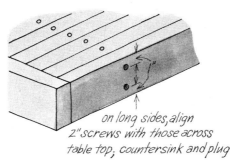

on long sides, align 2" screws with those across table top; countersink and plug

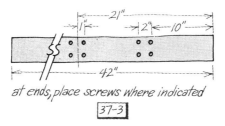

at ends, place screws where indicated

37-3

The next step is to notch the corners to receive the 4 by 4 legs. Measure the legs first—each should

be exactly 3½" by 3½". Then cut with a handsaw, sawing perpendicular to the top. Work carefully: these joints will show. Trim any rough edges with a chisel.

Clamp the legs in the notches. Mark and drill ½" holes for 8½" dowels as shown in drawing 37-4.

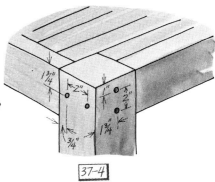

37-4

You may have to remove the legs to drill the holes deep enough.

Sand the top until it is flat and smooth, working in the same direction as the grain (for more about sanding, see page 74). Finally, apply Danish oil or polyurethane as a finish.

If a 1 by 2 warps sideways, apply a clamp at the point of warpage and drive 3-penny nails from the underside to hold it.

To cover the screws, cut wooden plugs from fir scraps with a plug-cutting bit.

Mark straight lines where the edges of the top should be. Then, with a handsaw or a circular saw and guide, trim off the excess wood. (For hints on cutting straight, see page 67.)

Cut the Common 2 by 4s to serve as a supporting frame beneath the plywood base. Screw them flat in place using 2" screws as detailed in drawing 37-2. Add a second frame

1X2s

¾" plywood

add 2x4 frame to underside

37-2

Corner leg detail is enhanced by dowel joinery.

Roll-around Bar

Countertop folds for mobility and storage.
See page 40.
Design: Donald Wm. MacDonald, AIA

Expandable Wine Rack

See facing page.
Design: Donald Wm. MacDonald, AIA

BAR & WINE RACK

Roll-around bar and modular wine rack—primarily plywood

Expandable Wine Rack

Photo on facing page

Some people buy wine by the bottle; others buy it by the case. The nice thing about this wine rack is that it's modular: depending upon the number of components you make, it will hold a few bottles or a cellar full.

TOOLS YOU'LL NEED: pencil · measuring tape · compass · square · saber saw · hammer · nailset (or large nail) · sandpaper and finishing tools. *Helpful tools* include a radial-arm or table saw, a dado blade, a large expansive bit, and a 1½" bit.

MATERIALS LIST (for unit shown):
½ sheet of A-A plywood (or equivalent)
1-pound box of 5d finishing nails
White glue
Wood filler
Enamel paint or clear finish

HERE'S HOW

You can cut the curves on the front of the rack in either of two ways. If you will be cutting the pieces to

size on your own radial-arm or table saw, consider marking the center points of the 1⅝" and ¾" radii first, drilling holes with an expansive bit and a 1½" bit at those marks, and then ripping the boards to size. (For the ¾" radius cuts, you can drill one series of three holes and rip down the center, using one half for one board and the other half for another.) By drilling instead of cutting the curves with a saw, you can make them truer.

If you have the major cuts made at the lumberyard, proceed as follows. Lay out and cut the half

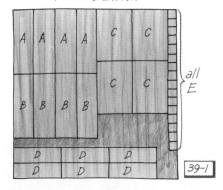

PLYWOOD LAYOUT

39-1

sheet of plywood as shown in drawing 39-1. Here are the sizes:
   (A) and (B) 6" by 18"
   (C) 10½" by 14½"
   (D) 4½" by 14"
   (E) 2" by 3¼" (see drawing 39-3)
   Using the pencil, measuring tape, square, and compass, lay out the cuts for all the notches and for the bottle openings as shown in drawing 39-2.
   Make the cuts with the saber saw. (See page 69 for information on cutting slots.)
   Glue and nail together the (A), (B), and (C) pieces as specified in

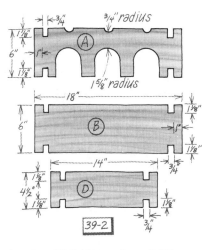

39-2

drawing 39-3. Then glue all (E) pieces in place. Set the nail heads below the surface and fill with wood filler. Also fill the plywood edges. Sand off any bumps, irregularities, and rough edges. Refill and sand again if necessary.

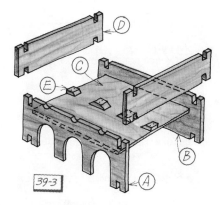

39-3

Assemble the wine rack by interlocking the components. Check for and make any necessary adjustments of the cuts. When all pieces fit properly, take them apart and paint them. Once the enamel dries, assemble everything again and stock it with wine bottles.

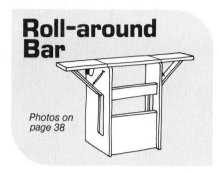

Roll-around Bar

Photos on page 38

This roll-around bar doesn't miss a move. As your party relocates from room to room, so does the bar. Its compact size and a set of four casters give it mobility. Then, when it's in place, the five-foot counter top unfolds for serving several guests at once.

Material expenses are minimal. The cart is made primarily from a single sheet of plywood and a hardwood chopping block.

Cutting out the plywood pieces is the toughest part of the project, but even this is easy if you have a radial-arm or table saw or a power circular saw with a guide (see page 68). Otherwise, you can have the lumberyard attendant make the major cuts.

TOOLS YOU'LL NEED: pencil · measuring tape · square · compass · straightedge · saber saw (with guide) · hacksaw · handsaw · chisel · drill · ⅛" and ½" bits · C-clamps · hammer · nailset (or large nail) · screwdriver · sandpaper and finishing tools. *Helpful tools* include a radial-arm or table saw or a power circular saw.

MATERIALS LIST:
1 sheet of ¾" A-A (or birch) plywood
2' of 1 by 10
2' of 1 by 12
1 hardwood chopping block, 1' by 5'
6 L-brackets
4 casters with screws
4 shelf brackets with clips and screws
6 fixed-pin butt hinges, 2", with ¾" screws
2' of continuous hinge, ¾"
24 flathead screws, ¾" by #5
2 each of screw-on hooks, ¼" eyebolts, turnbuckles
2 wooden cabinet knobs (or equivalent)
1 roll heavy cord, colored
1-pound box of 6d finishing nails
White glue
Wood filler
Enamel paint
Vegetable oil

HERE'S HOW

Lay out the plywood cuts as shown in drawing 40-1. Be sure to use a square for precise marking. Here are the sizes:

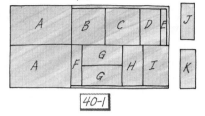

¾" A-A plywood

40-1

(A) 24" x 37"
(B) 22½" by 20½"
(C) 22½" by 20½"
(D) 22½" by 12¾"
(E) 22½" by 4"
(F) 22½" by 6½"
(G) 11¼" by 24¼"
(H) 22½" by 12"
(I) 22½" by 16"
(J) ¾" by 10" by 22½" (use plywood or a 1 by 12)
(K) ¾" by 9¼" by 22" (use plywood or a 1 by 10)

Some lumberyards carry chopping blocks in standard sizes; the one shown was purchased from a cabinetmaker. It's wise to have the lumberyard people or the cabinetmaker cut it precisely into its three sections *after* you've built the cart.

Start with the side panels (A). See drawing for keyed parts. Using a saber saw, cut the handle holes and top-support brackets as shown in drawings 40-2 and 40-3. Begin the

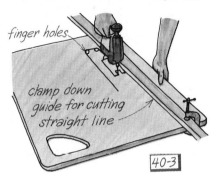

finger holes

clamp down guide for cutting straight line

40-3

handle-hole cuts from ½" holes drilled in the waste wood; start the support bracket cuts from the 1" finger holes specified.

Duplicate the marks shown in drawing 40-2 onto the inside

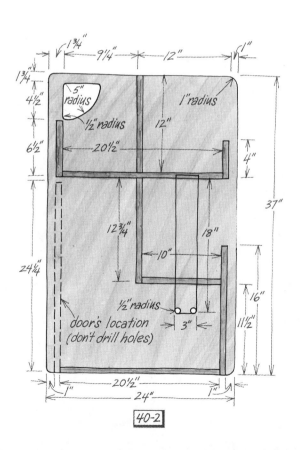

5" radius
½" radius
1" radius
12"
20½"
12¾"
10"
18"
½" radius
door's location (don't drill holes)
3"
37"
4"
16"
11½"
1¾"
9¼"
12"
1"
1¾"
4½"
6½"
24¼"
20½"
24"
1"
1"

40-2

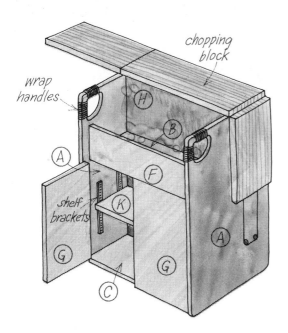
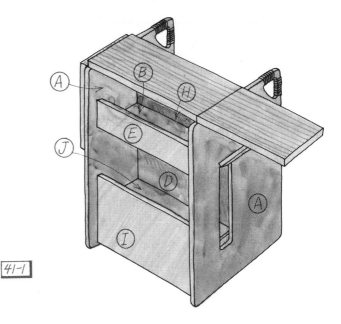

chopping block

wrap handles

shelf brackets

41-1

surface of one of the side panels (A). Clamp that panel to its mate, flush at all edges, and drill ⅛" holes every 4" between the lines, penetrating both panels. Put a scrap beneath the lower panel so you don't break away the wood or drill into your work surface. Be sure to drill the holes straight (see page 70).

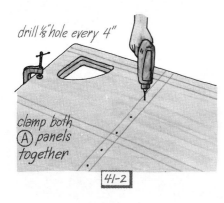

drill ⅛"hole every 4"

clamp both (A) panels together

41-2

Drilling the holes into the lower panel eliminates the need for marking that panel and makes nailing easier. After drilling all the holes, unclamp the pieces and set the unmarked panel aside.

Glue and nail piece (C) to the marked side panel (A). For fastening all permanent shelves and dividers to the cabinet, use glue and 6-penny finishing nails, setting the nail heads below the surface. Glue

and nail piece (I) to (A) and (C). Put a ¾" block beneath it as shown in drawing 41-3 to raise the level slightly and make nailing easier.

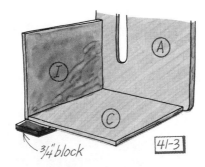

¾" block

41-3

Glue and nail piece (J) to (A) and (I); then glue and nail piece (D) to (A) and (J). Glue and nail piece (B) to (A) and (D). Next, glue and toenail the outer edge of piece (H) to (B); then nail piece (D) to (A). Add pieces (E) and (F). Set all nails.

Lay the unit on its side and spread glue along all the exposed edges of shelves and dividers; then lay the other side panel (A) into position and nail it. Set all the nail heads and wipe away any excess glue.

Attach the two support flaps, using butt hinges as shown in drawing 41-4. Cut the continuous hinge into two 12" pieces and screw them in place with ¾" by #5 flathead screws, as shown in drawing 41-4.

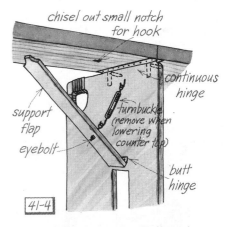

chisel out small notch for hook

continuous hinge

support flap

turnbuckle (remove when lowering counter top)

eyebolt

butt hinge

41-4

Attach the top temporarily, using L-brackets (you may want to remove the top when painting the unit). Add the turnbuckle flap supports, also shown. Screw the furniture casters to the bottom of the unit, setting them in about 1" from all edges; fasten the shelf brackets inside the unit for the shelf (K); and hinge the doors (G) on the front, using butt hinges. You can either add knobs for door pulls or drill finger holes.

Sand and paint the unit, being careful not to get paint on the chopping block top. Apply a coat of vegetable oil to the block. Then spiral the handles with heavy cord or leather thonging; tack or glue it in place or knot it in drilled holes at each end.

BEDS

From standard softwood, bunk beds and a double bed

Bolt-together Bunk Beds

Photo on facing page

Leaving tradition behind, these contemporary bunk beds offer two children an exciting environment for play and sleeping.

And, because they simply bolt together, making these bunks requires only basic tools and techniques.

TOOLS YOU'LL NEED: pencil · measuring tape · square · handsaw · drill · $^{13}⁄_{64}$", $^{3}⁄_{8}$", 1", 1¼" bits, #9 by 2" screw pilot · hammer (or mallet) · screwdriver · $^{7}⁄_{16}$" socket and handle · sandpaper and finishing tools. *Helpful tools* include a radial-arm saw, table saw, or power circular saw, a dado blade, a drill press, and a power sander.

MATERIALS LIST:

45' of 2 by 6 Clear fir
57' of 2 by 3 Clear fir
39' of 1 by 2 Clear fir
26' of 1" doweling
4' of 1¼" doweling
2 sheets of ½" shop-grade plywood
18 lag screws, ¼" by 3½"
14 carriage bolts, ¼" by 2"
12 carriage bolts, ¼" by 3"
44 washers, ¼"
26 nuts, ¼"
44 flathead screws, 2" by #9
White glue
Wood filler
Clear polyurethane finish
Two mattresses, 6" by 39" by 75"

HERE'S HOW

The unit pictured is for mattresses 6" by 39" by 75". You can modify the plans to fit slightly smaller or larger mattresses. When making the bed frames, figure your mattress size plus 1" in length and width for blankets.

Begin by cutting the various pieces to size, according to the following list of sizes, keyed to drawing 43-1. Mark and check your cuts with a square.

(A) Two 2 by 6s, 91¾"
(B) Two 2 by 6s, 40"
(C) Two 2 by 6s, 76"
(D) One 2 by 6, 43"
(E) One 2 by 6, 59"
(F) One 2 by 6, 17½"
(G) Four 2 by 3s, 71"
(H) One 2 by 3, 60"
(I) One 2 by 3, 48" (optional)
(J) One 2 by 3, 67½"
(K) One 2 x 3, 71½"
(L) One 2 by 3, 46"
(M) Two 2 by 3s, 20"
(N) One 2 by 3, 43"
(O) Fifteen 1" dowels, 9½"
(P) Five 1" dowels, 16"
(Q) One 1¼" dowel, 43"
(R) Four 1 by 2s, 38½"
(S) Four 1 by 2s, 76"
(T) Two ½" plywood pieces, 40" by 76"

Also cut seventy 1"-long plugs from the 1"-diameter doweling for plugging the bolt holes. You need two for each carriage bolt and one for each lag screw.

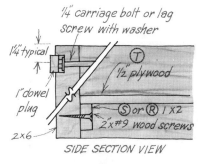

SIDE SECTION VIEW

42-1

Almost all parts of the bed are either bolted together or fastened with lag screws. Where you bolt through the edge of a 2 by 3 to the flat side of a 2 by 6 or a 2 by 3, use 3" bolts. Where you bolt together the flat sides of two 2 by 6s or 2 by 3s, use 2" bolts. Drill ⅜"

bolt holes for the ¼" bolts in order to allow for slight discrepancies in alignment.

To join the flat side of one 2 by 6 or 2 by 3 to the end of another, use lag screws. Counterbore their heads for plugs the same way you do the bolts (drawing 42-1). For ¼" lag screws, drill $^{13}⁄_{64}$" pilot holes.

Typical spacing of bolts and lag screws across the 2 by 6s is shown in detail drawing 42-2.

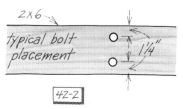

42-2

Drill the 1¼"-diameter closet-pole holes and counterbore holes 1" in diameter by ⅝" deep for lag screws.

Knock the closet pole (Q) into its holes. Place both (B) 2 by 6s between the (A) 2 by 6s where specified in drawing 43-1, and drill $^{13}⁄_{64}$" pilot holes through (A) and into (B) for the lag screws. Lag-screw both (A) pieces to both (B) pieces.

Next bolt together the other bed frame (C, D, and E) the same way.

Making the ladder is next. Mark two (G) 2 by 3s for all the 1"-diameter holes for dowel rungs (P) where specified in drawing 43-1. Drill the holes, dab a little glue into each, and knock the dowels (P) into the holes of one 2 by 3 (G). Pound the second 2 by 3 onto the dowels, using a wooden mallet or a hammer and a wood block. The two 2 by 3s (G) should be parallel, spaced 13".

In the bed shown in the photograph, (F) is interlocking and bolted to (D). You needn't go to the labor of cutting the interlocking joint; you can simply bolt (F) to (D).

Drill the bolt holes in all the (G) and (H) 2 by 3s and bolt them to the lower bed frame. Then drill the corresponding bolt holes in (A), and the holes for the 1"-diameter railing dowel (O) in (A) and (B).

Have a friend help you lift and

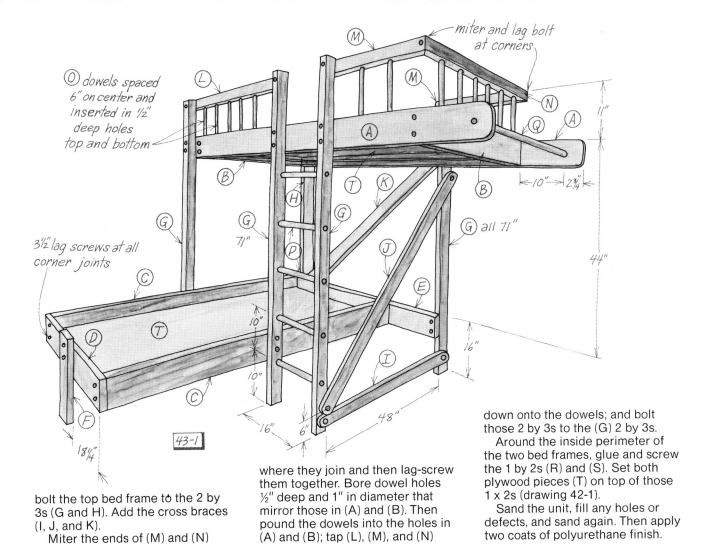

(O) dowels spaced 6" on center and inserted in ½" deep holes top and bottom

(L)

(M)

(M)

miter and lag bolt at corners

(N)

11"

(A)

(Q)

(A)

(B)

(T)

(K)

(G)

(B)

←10"→ 2¾"

(H)

(G)

(G) all 71"

71"

(P)

(J)

44"

3½" lag screws at all corner joints

(C)

(E)

(D)

(T)

(G)

10"

16"

(I)

43-1

(C)

16"

6"

48"

(F)

18¼"

bolt the top bed frame to the 2 by 3s (G and H). Add the cross braces (I, J, and K).

Miter the ends of (M) and (N)

where they join and then lag-screw them together. Bore dowel holes ½" deep and 1" in diameter that mirror those in (A) and (B). Then pound the dowels into the holes in (A) and (B); tap (L), (M), and (N)

down onto the dowels; and bolt those 2 by 3s to the (G) 2 by 3s.

Around the inside perimeter of the two bed frames, glue and screw the 1 by 2s (R) and (S). Set both plywood pieces (T) on top of those 1 x 2s (drawing 42-1).

Sand the unit, fill any holes or defects, and sand again. Then apply two coats of polyurethane finish.

Bolt-together Bunk Beds
See facing page. Design: John Schmid, Architect

Double Bed with Storage

Would you believe that you could make this handsome bed with no tools more sophisticated than a hammer and a handsaw? You can. And because the frame is made from standard softwoods, it is quite inexpensive. In addition, the bed offers a bonus: two compartments at the foot of the bed provide roomy storage.

Though the bed shown is sized for a standard double-bed mattress, you can revise the dimensions for a larger mattress. Allow 1" on all sides for blankets.

TOOLS YOU'LL NEED: pencil · measuring tape · square · handsaw · drill · ¾" bit, #10 by 1¼" screw pilot, plug cutter · hammer · screwdriver · sandpaper and finishing tools. *Helpful tools* include a power sander and a radial-arm saw, table saw, or power circular saw.

MATERIALS LIST:

2 sheets of ¾" shop grade plywood
½ sheet (24" by 96") of ¼" tempered
  hardboard
29' of 1 by 8 fir
41' of 1 by 2 fir
20' of 2 by 8 fir
10' of ½" by ½" molding
1 box (100) flathead screws, 1¼" by #10
1-pound box of 5d finishing nails
1-pound box of 16d finishing nails
Wood filler
White glue
53" by 76" of 8"-thick foam (or double-
  bed mattress)
Enamel paint or other finish

HERE'S HOW

Begin by cutting the pieces to size according to the following schedule, keyed to drawing 45-1. Use a square to mark and check your cuts. (For more about cutting, see page 67.)

    (A) Two 2 by 8s, 69"
    (B) Two 2 by 8s, 45"
    (C) Two 1 by 8s, 87¼"
    (D) Three 1 by 8s, 55"

    (E) Two pieces ¾" plywood, 27½"
        by 76"
    (F) Two pieces ¼" hardboard, 9"
        by 55"
    (G) Two 1 by 2s, 76"
    (H) Four 1 by 2s, 53½"
    (I) Three 1 by 2s, 42"
    (J) Two ½" by ½" pieces, 55"

Attach the (A) and (B) pieces for the bed's base with butt joints by gluing them and nailing with 16-penny nails. Use the square to check for true 90° corners. Sand any irregularities.

Next, assemble the 1 by 8 frame that goes around the mattress, using glue and screws to make butt joints. Drill pilot holes for three 1¼" by #10 screws per joint. Before attaching the 1 by 8 at the foot of the storage compartment, glue and nail with 5-penny nails the ½" by ½" moldings (J) and the 1 by 2s (H) that attach the compartment bottom to the 1 by 8s, placed as shown in detail drawing 44-1.

Glue and screw (with 1¼" screws every 12") the 1 by 2s, (G) and (H), around the lower inside rim of the 1 by 8 frame. Also nail (I) across the center where specified and the remaining (H) 1 by 2s.

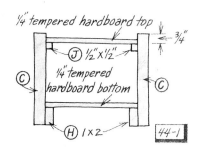

Lay the two plywood pieces inside the frame, resting them on top of the 1 by 2s (G and H). Drill pilot holes and screw the plywood in place with six 1¼" screws spaced evenly along each side and three screws along each end.

Set this frame on the base. Fasten with six 1¼" screws.

Next, glue the bottom into the storage compartment. Then measure and mark across the middle of the storage compartment's lid. Cut it in half and drill ¾" finger holes where shown.

Fill any holes or mistakes and sand; repeat if necessary. Sand the entire bed, excluding the hardboard surfaces. Wipe clean and apply two coats of enamel.

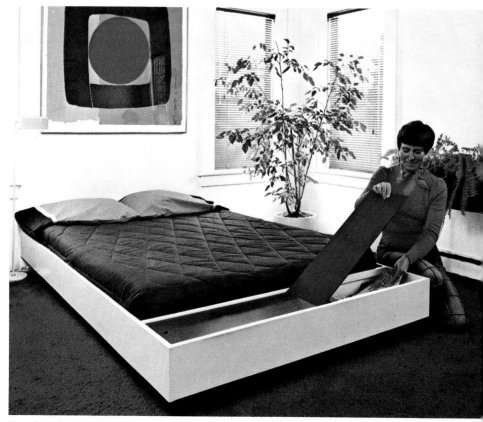

Double Bed with Storage   *Design: Roger H. Newell, AIA*

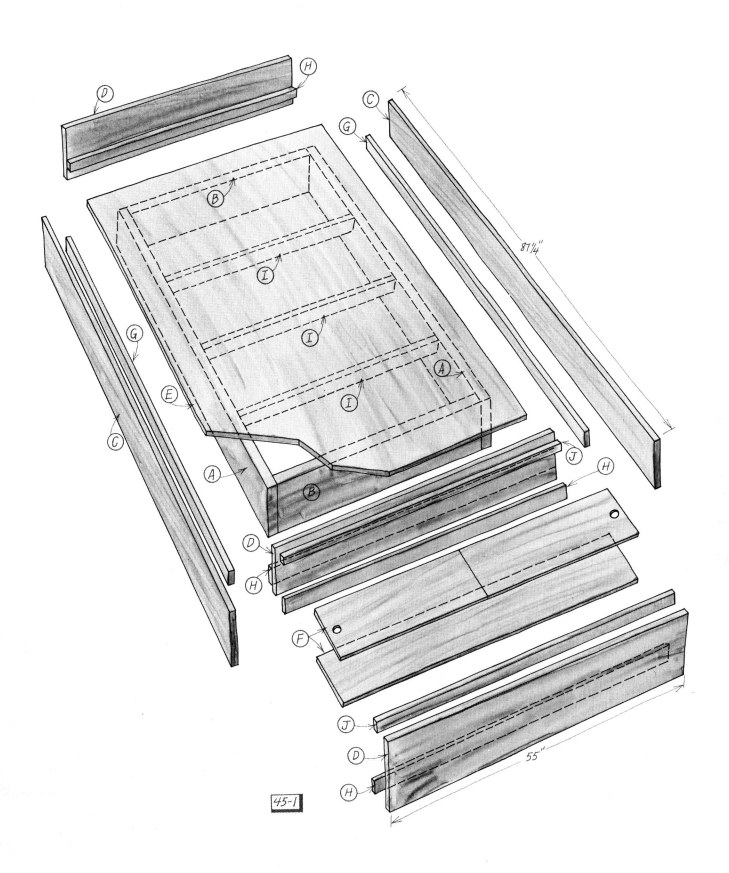

45-1

BEDROOM FURNISHINGS

Pine headboard, storage seat, and chest of drawers

Chest of Drawers, Headboard, and Storage Seat   *Design: Donald Wm. MacDonald, AIA*

Drawer sides are made from 1 by 4s for easy sliding.

Chest of Drawers

Photo on facing page

This pine chest of drawers is designed to be made from standard 1 by 12s and 1 by 4s, plywood, and moldings. You simply cut out the pieces and glue and nail them together.

Of course, you can alter the design if you like—particularly the depth of the drawers. Some large drawers are difficult to slide. To avoid that problem, we've made the sides and backs of this chest's drawers only 3½" tall. This makes the drawers easy to operate, but they won't hold as much as taller ones. If you prefer the added storage capacity, consider substituting 1 by 6s, 1 by 8s, or even 1 by 10s for the 1 by 4 drawer sides and backs. But if you do this, be sure to make the necessary adjustments when buying materials and when placing the drawer slides.

Another suggestion: this chest of drawers is quite tall—more than 5' —and quite deep. If you wish to scale it down, substitute 1 by 10s for all the 1 by 12s and make the necessary adjustments for these substitutions in your materials list and working measurements.

TOOLS YOU'LL NEED: pencil · measuring tape · square · compass · coping saw or saber saw · handsaw · hammer · nailset (or large nail) · pipe or bar clamps · sandpaper and finishing tools. *Helpful tools* include a radial-arm or table saw and a power sander.

MATERIALS LIST:

37' of 1 by 12 Clear pine
44' of 1 by 4 pine, #2 Common
1 sheet of ¼" A-D plywood
48' of ¾" by ¾" molding
14' of ½" by ¾" pine molding
1-pound box of 3d finishing nails
1-pound box of 5d finishing nails
White glue
Wood filler
Clear polyurethane finish
Dark brown enamel paint

HERE'S HOW

Because the height of the chest of drawers is determined by the width of the 1 by 12 boards used for drawer fronts, measure your 1 by 12s before you cut the side panels (E) to length. Standard 1 by 12s measure 11¼"; these plans are based on that measurement.

Cut the pieces to size according to the following schedule, keyed to drawing 47-1. (For more information on cutting, see page 67.) Mark and check your cuts with a combination square.

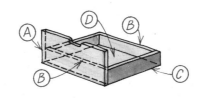

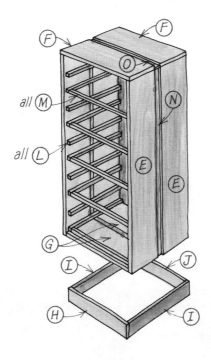

47-1

(A) Five 1 by 12s, 22⅜"
(B) Ten 1 by 4s, 20¹³⁄₁₆"
(C) Ten 1 by 4s, 22"
(D) Five pieces of ¼" plywood, 22" by 22⁵⁄₁₆"
(E) Four 1 by 12s, 57⅜"
(F) Two 1 by 12s, 24"
(G) Two 1 by 12s, 22½"
(H) One 1 by 4, 20"
(I) Two 1 by 4s, 19½"
(J) One 1 by 4, 18½"
(K) One piece ¼" plywood, 23½" by 57½"
(L) Twenty pieces ¾" by ¾" molding, 22⁹⁄₁₆"
(M) Five pieces ¾" by ¾" molding, 21"
(N) Two ½" by ¾" pieces, 56⅞"
(O) Two ½" by ¾" pieces, 23⁹⁄₁₆"

As you can see in drawing 47-1, the chest's sides (E), top (F), and bottom (G) are each made from a pair of 1 by 12s glued to a ¾" by ½" spacer. Before joining the three pieces for each surface, paint the face of the ½" by ¾" spacer dark brown.

When the paint dries, form a single slab from the two 1 by 12s and the spacer as follows. Spread glue along one edge of each 1 by 12 and along both ½" edges of the molding. Working on a flat surface, place the molding between the 1 by 12s, flush with what is to be the cabinet's inner surface. At three or four points along the slab's length, apply slight pressure with bar or pipe clamps (slip a wood scrap under the clamp jaws to protect the pine). Wipe off excess glue. Until the glue dries, make sure that the boards stay flat, keeping them from buckling or bowing under the pressure of the clamps.

Next, assemble the drawers according to drawing 47-1. Do this by gluing and nailing the (B) and (C) pieces together, then gluing and nailing the ¼" plywood bottoms (D) in place. Nail the plywood with 3-penny finishing nails; make the corner joints with 5-penny finishing nails.

Use the compass and measuring tape to mark the handle holes on the (A) pieces as specified in drawing 47-2. Cut these with a coping saw or saber saw and sand them smooth.

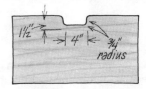

47-2

1½"   4"   ¾" radius

(Continued on page 48)

... *Continued from page 47*

Then glue and nail (B) pieces to (A) pieces with 3-penny finishing nails, *nailing from the inside of the drawer.* Set all nail heads about $\frac{1}{16}$" below the surface.

Now, using a square, mark on the inside faces of (E) for placement of the runners (L) for the bottom of each drawer (see drawing 48-1).

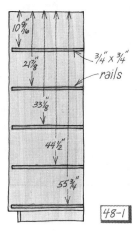

Fasten the runners with 3-penny finishing nails, setting the heads. Repeat for the other side (E).

Have someone help you hold the sides (E) up on edge now while you glue and nail the top (F) and bottom (G) to them. Use 5-penny nails and set the heads.

Apply the back (K) with glue and 3-penny nails to make the cabinet rigid and square. The back should inset $\frac{1}{4}$" from the chest's top and sides.

Glue and nail together the base—pieces (H), (I), and (J)—as illustrated in drawing 47-1 (page 47), using 5-penny nails and setting the heads.

Now set the cabinet box on the base and nail it in place with 5-penny nails.

Slide the bottom drawer in on its runners. Glue and nail runners over the top edge of both drawer sides, attaching the runners to sides (E) with 3-penny finishing nails. Allow about $\frac{1}{16}$" for easy drawer movement. Repeat this installation of top runners for the remaining drawers.

Fill any exposed nail holes or defects, and sand the entire unit until smooth. Wipe away all sawdust. Apply two coats of dark brown enamel to the base and two coats of clear polyurethane to the remainder. To insure smooth drawer movement, buff the runners with fine steel wool.

Headboard

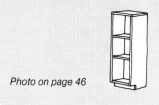

Photo on page 46

Bedside storage and a comfortable means of propping yourself up for nighttime reading is what this easy-to-make headboard offers. It's actually composed of two cabinet boxes, with adjustable shelves, that stand on each side of the bed; cushions hang from a 1 by 4 that joins the two cabinets. Depending upon cushion sizes and the 1 by 4's length, the headboard will fit any bed, from single to king size.

TOOLS YOU'LL NEED: pencil · measuring tape · square · handsaw · drill · $\frac{1}{4}$" bit · hammer · nailset (or large nail) · sandpaper and finishing tools · sewing equipment.
Helpful tools include a radial-arm or table saw, a drill press, and a power sander. Although not required, a sewing machine will save you hours.

MATERIALS LIST:

22' of 1 by 12 Clear pine
3' of 1 by 4
One Clear pine 1 by 4, your bed's width plus 30"
$\frac{1}{2}$ sheet (48" by 48") of $\frac{1}{4}$" A-D plywood
16 shelf pegs, $\frac{1}{4}$"
1-pound box of 5d finishing nails
1-pound box of 2d finishing nails
White glue
Wood filler
Clear polyurethane finish
Dark brown enamel paint
$3\frac{1}{2}$ yards of 36", 45", or 54" fabric or $1\frac{3}{4}$ yards of 60" fabric (If you want cushions larger or smaller than the queen-size cushions shown in this design, be sure to make the necessary adjustments.)
Matching polyester thread
8 yards of polyester batting
8 shelf pins, $\frac{1}{4}$"
Thumbtacks

HERE'S HOW

Begin by cutting the pieces to the following sizes, according to drawing 48-2. (For more about cutting see page 67.) Be sure to use a square to mark and check your cuts.

(A) Four 1 by 12s, $39\frac{1}{4}$"
(B) Two 1 by 12s (ripped to $10\frac{1}{2}$" wide), 16"
(C) Two 1 by 12s, $14\frac{1}{2}$"
(D) Four 1 by 12s, $14\frac{3}{8}$"
(E) Two pieces $\frac{1}{4}$" plywood, $15\frac{1}{2}$" by 36"
(F) Two 1 by 4s, 16"

Remember that these pieces make two bedside cabinets, not just one. With this in mind, divide them up—half for one cabinet, half for the other. The following instructions will tell you how to make one cabinet; just duplicate them for the other.

First mark all cuts with a pencil and square. Using the handsaw, cut the $3\frac{1}{2}$" by 3" toe space from the bottom front corner of both (A) pieces. Then cut the $\frac{3}{4}$" by $3\frac{1}{2}$" notch for the pillow-supporting 1 by

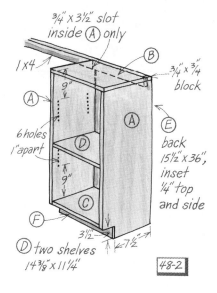

4 into the top back corner of only one (A) piece. (For more about cutting slots, see page 69.) Remember that this notch must be cut in the *right* side of one cabinet and in the *left* side of the other.

To form the basic cabinet box, glue and nail with 5-penny finishing nails the sides (A) to the top (B) and to the 1 by 4 at the base (F). Attach the back (E) with glue and 2-penny finishing nails, recessing it $\frac{1}{4}$" from the sides and the top.

Set all nails that will show, fill the holes, and sand smooth. Refill and sand again if necessary.

Mark and drill holes $\frac{1}{4}$" in diameter and $\frac{1}{2}$" deep for shelf pins where specified. Insert shelf pins; set shelves (D) on them when the cabinet is completely finished.

If you haven't cut the pillow-supporting 1 by 4 to length yet, do so now. Sand all wood pieces.

Paint the front of the toe space dark brown; finish the rest of the wood with clear polyurethane. For an interesting contrast, consider painting the front of the cabinet back (E) dark brown as well; this is easiest to do before attaching it.

To make each cushion, start by folding one 60" by 28" fabric rectangle in half across the short dimension. Then, with right sides together, stitch along both long edges, allowing ½" for seams.

Cut the batting to two 4-yard by 21" sections, one for stuffing each cushion. Fold each section in a rolling motion to form a block about 7" by 19" by 21" and overcast-stitch the loose end to the block. Turn the fabric cover right side out, press it, and stuff it with the batting. Thumb-tack each cushion and wind it around the 1 by 4 as shown in drawing 49-1.

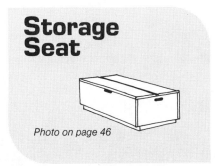

For illustrations of the principal steps in making these cushions, see "How to make a knife-edge cushion," page 78.

Storage Seat

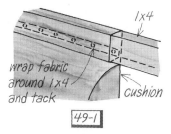

Photo on page 46

Part of the matching set shown on page 46, this storage chest keeps linens and extra blankets within easy reach of the bed. It's made like a box with a hinged lid. By changing the dimensions, you can make the chest so its length matches any bed width; the one shown is for a queen-size bed.

TOOLS YOU'LL NEED: pencil · measuring tape · square · compass · coping or saber saw · handsaw · hammer · nailset (or large nail) · screwdriver · sandpaper and finishing tools. *Helpful tools* include a radial-arm or table saw and a power sander.

MATERIALS LIST:

21' of 1 by 10 Clear pine
13' of 1 by 12 Clear pine
1 sheet of ¼" A-D plywood
12' of 1 by 4
10' of ½" by ¾" molding
5' of continuous hinge, with screws
1-pound box of 5d finishing nails
1-pound box of ¾" finishing nails
White glue
Wood filler
Clear polyurethane finish
Dark brown enamel paint

HERE'S HOW

If possible, have the lumberyard cut the ¼" plywood sheet to give two pieces 16½" by 58⅜". Also, if you want your cabinet exactly the size shown in drawing 49-2, the 1 by 10s must be ripped to 8⅝" widths. If you don't have a table saw or a radial-arm saw for this, find out if the lumberyard attendant can do it. If not, make the cabinet 19¼" wide instead of 18". (For more about cutting, see page 67.)

Assuming that you've succeeded in getting the 1 by 10s ripped to 8⅝", proceed as follows. Otherwise, make the necessary adjustments for a larger top and wider cabinet.

First cut the various pieces to size according to the following list; it's keyed to drawing 49-2. Use a square to mark and check your cuts.

(A) Two 1 by 10s (ripped to 8⅝" wide), 5'
(B) Two 1 by 10s (ripped to 8⅝" wide), 58½"
(C) Two 1 by 12s, 5'
(D) Two 1 by 12s, 16½"
(E) Two 1 by 4s, 56"
(F) Two 1 by 4s, 13½"
(G) Two pieces of ¼" plywood, 16½" by 58½" (Cut these now if they were not cut at the lumberyard.)
(H) One piece ½" by ¾" molding, 5'
(I) One piece ½" by ¾" molding, 58½"

Lay boards (A) and (B), in pairs, face down on a flat surface; space each pair ¾" apart with its ¾" by ½" strip. Make sure that the boards and the strip are flush at both ends. Glue and nail one ¼" plywood piece (good side up) to both boards of each pair. Use ¾" finishing nails.

With a square and compass, mark the handle holes for (C) and (D) as detailed in drawing 49-2. Then cut them out, using a saber saw or coping saw.

Next, have a friend help you hold the (C) and (D) pieces together while you glue and nail them at the corners according to drawing 49-2. Use 5-penny finishing nails, setting the heads. Also glue and nail together the base, pieces (E) and (F).

Paint the decorative ¾" by ½" strips brown, let them dry, and glue them in place. Then glue and nail piece (B) to the (C) and (D) assembly. Space 5-penny nails about 6" apart, setting the heads.

Join the top (A) to the back (C) with the continuous hinge. Use a nailset to punch starting holes for the screws.

Fill all nail holes and defects and sand; repeat if necessary. After sanding the entire unit until it's very smooth, apply dark brown enamel paint to the base and clear polyure-thane to the rest of the chest.

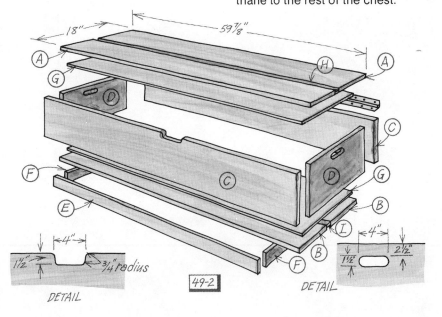

CHILDREN'S FURNITURE

Fun and functional plywood modules for kids

Rockers, arches, tables, stools, chairs: all come from three basic components. These simple, functional pieces of children's furniture open worlds of exploration, adventure, and creativity for kids. They become what the children make them. Each piece can be turned on any edge or surface to become something new and different. And, like life-size building blocks, they're easy to stack or join in any configuration so kids can create their own environments.

From one sheet of plywood and some closet-pole rounds, you can make nine of the square or rectangular units or three of the large, rocking curved units.

TOOLS YOU'LL NEED: pencil · measuring tape · square · compass · straightedge · saber saw · handsaw · drill · expansive bit · hammer or mallet · sandpaper and finishing tools. *Helpful tools* include a radial-arm or table saw or a power circular saw, a drill press, and a power sander.

MATERIALS LIST:
2 sheets of ¾" birch plywood
105 feet of 1⅜"-diameter closet-pole rounds
White glue
Wood filler
Clear polyurethane finish or bright colors of lead-free enamel paint

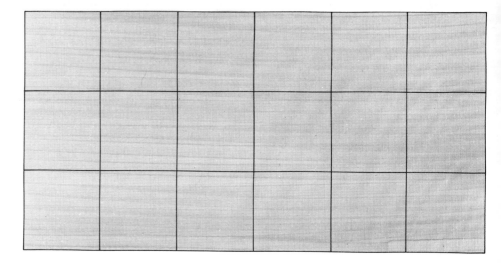

PLYWOOD LAYOUTS

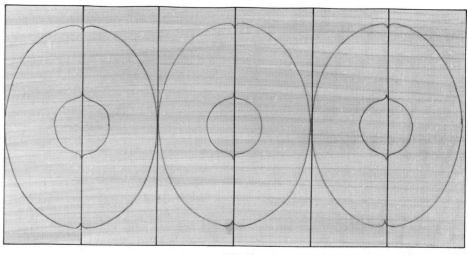

50-1

HERE'S HOW

If possible, have lumberyard personnel make the main cuts across the plywood. (See drawing 50-1.)

For the large, rounded pieces, mark the radii as shown in drawing 51-1. If you'll be dividing up the plywood at home, make these marks before cutting out the sections. If you have the major cuts made at the lumberyard, you'll have to clamp the plywood firmly to a work surface and tack the yardstick to a ¾" block as shown in drawing 51-2.

Before cutting any of the curves, lay out all the other lines for the holes. Remember that half of the pieces are the mirror image of the other half. Also lay out the lines for the square pieces, including the rounded corners.

Cut along the straight lines with a handsaw, and use the saber saw to cut the curves.

(Continued on page 52)

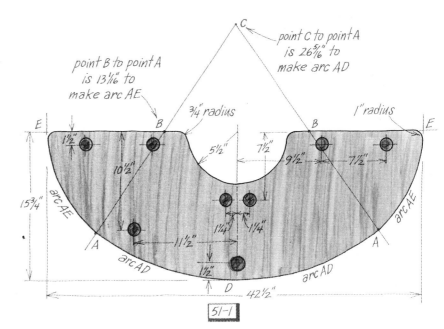

point B to point A is 13¹/₁₆" to make arc AE

point C to point A is 26⁵/₁₆" to make arc AD

¾" radius
1" radius
5½"
7½"
10½"
15¾"
9½"
7½"
1¼"
1¼"
11½"
1½"
arc AE
arc AD
42½"

51-1

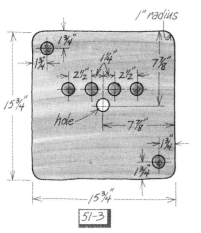

tack to work surface

¾"-thick wood block

pencil

yardstick

42½"

15¾"

51-2

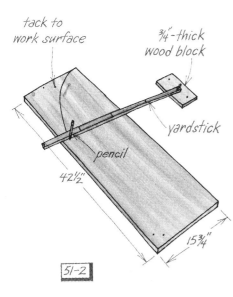

1" radius

1¾"
1¼"
2½" 2½"
7⅞"
15¾"
hole
7⅞"
1¾"
1¾"
15¾"

51-3

Children's Furniture   *Design: Maynard Hale Lyndon, Placemakers/Cambridge*

Exploring, creating, working, playing: children love these fun furniture pieces. The three easy-to-make modules become desks, chairs, benches, rockers, bridges, and anything else a child's imagination can create.

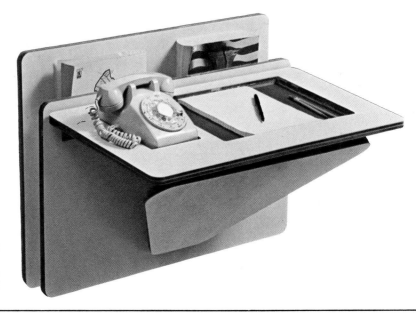

Telephone Desk

See facing page.
Design: Donald Wm. MacDonald, AIA

Sewing Center

Front door folds down for work surface.
See page 56.
Design: Donald Wm. MacDonald, AIA

ACTIVITY CENTERS

Telephone desk hangs on wall; sewing center folds down

Telephone Desk

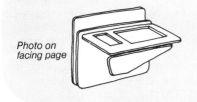

Photo on facing page

What could be more convenient than a small wall-hung desk with room for phone books, the telephone, and a writing tablet? This project, easy to make from plywood and 1 by 3s, fills the order.

TOOLS YOU'LL NEED: pencil · measuring tape · square · compass · saber saw · hammer · nailset (or large nail) · screwdriver · sandpaper and finishing tools. *A helpful tool* would be a radial-arm or table saw.

MATERIALS LIST:
1 sheet of ¾" A-A (or birch) plywood
8' of 1 by 3 pine or fir
5 button-tip hinges (removable pins), 2½"
Enough ¾" screws for the hinges
1-pound box of 3d finishing nails
1-pound box of 5d finishing nails
1-pound box of 8d finishing nails
White glue
Wood filler
Enamel paint

HERE'S HOW

Begin by cutting the following rectangles from the plywood sheet. Use a square to mark and check all cuts, and be sure to allow for the saw cut (kerf) when laying out the pieces. (For more about cutting, see page 67.)
   (A) 30" by 22"

(B) 30" by 18"
(C) 30" by 16"
(D) 26" by 14"
(E) 26" by 18"
   Further lay out and cut the (E) piece as shown in drawing 55-1. Using the saber saw, round the corners of all pieces as specified in drawings 55-3 and 56-1 (next page).
   Then cut the 1 by 3s to length for the frame. You'll need two pieces 24½" long, two 14" long, and one 6¼" long.

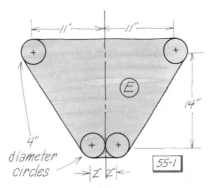

Using glue and 5-penny finishing nails, assemble the 1 by 3 frame as

shown in drawing 55-3. Set the nail heads slightly below the surface. Then, using the square, check that the corners are true 90.°
   Mark the frame's placement on piece (A). Spread glue along the edges of one side of the frame and fasten it to (A) by nailing from the backside of (A) with 5-penny nails.

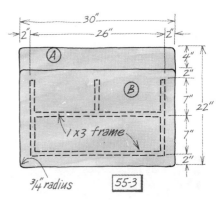

Next cut the rectangular holes in piece (C), using the saber saw. (For more about making a cutout, see

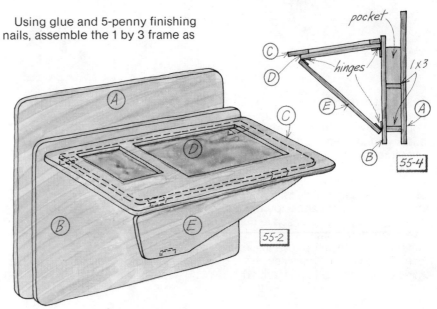

TELEPHONE DESK **55**

"How to make a cutout," page 68.)

Fasten piece (C) to piece (D), using glue and nailing from the backside of (D) with 3-penny finishing nails. Set the nail heads slightly.

Fill all nail holes and any holes in the plywood edges, sand smooth, and paint. For an interesting contrast, paint piece (D) a different color than the other pieces.

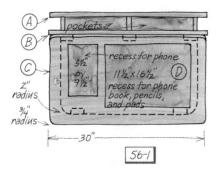

56-1

Then use the hinges to attach (D) to (E), (E) to (B), and (D) to (B), in that order.

Last, nail the unit to wall studs (through the wall covering), using several 8-penny finishing nails. Make sure that the desk is level and at a comfortable height; about 28" off the floor is right for most people.

Sewing Center

Photos on page 54

To unfold this well-organized sewing center from its tidy cabinet, you simply open the bottom doors and swing the second door down until it rests on them.

This unfolding creates a sewing work counter and exposes thread storage and small shelves. Behind the large door above the counter is room for fabric storage; above that, two doors hide patterns, books, or other supplies. You can use the area behind the bottom doors as a hamper for articles to be mended.

To open the counter, you must *always* open the bottom doors first. If you don't like this restriction, consider departing slightly from the design shown. Instead of resting the counter on the doors, with slots corresponding to door-top tabs, eliminate these and support the counter at each end with a small chain or folding bracket. If you use this support method, you can also eliminate the casters at the base of the bottom doors.

TOOLS YOU'LL NEED: pencil · measuring tape · square · compass · saber saw · handsaw · hacksaw · drill · ¼" and ¾" bits · hammer · nailset (or large nail) · screwdriver · sandpaper and finishing tools. *Helpful tools* include a radial-arm saw, table saw, or power circular saw.

MATERIALS LIST:
2½ sheets of ¾" A-A (or birch) plywood
1 sheet of ¾" A-D plywood
5' of ¼" doweling
1' of 2 by 2
2 casters with screws
12' of continuous hinge with ¾" screws
1-pound box of 6d finishing nails
White glue
Wood filler
Enamel paint or polyurethane finish

HERE'S HOW

Begin by cutting the various pieces of plywood to size, as specified in drawing 56-2. If possible, have the major cuts made at the lumberyard.

Assemble the sides, back, top, and bottom of the cabinet, using glue and 6-penny finishing nails, according to drawing 57-1. Also glue and nail the shelves and shelf dividers in place. Set the nail heads.

The next job, and the most difficult, is to cut the doors from the piece of plywood that goes on the cabinet's front. You must do this very carefully; any mistakes you make will show on the finished unit as gaps between the doors and the face frame. So first lay out all cutting lines for doors as specified in drawing 57-1.

Note that each handle hole, as well as the two slots on the counter's underside, has a ¾" hole bored at each end. These holes serve two purposes: they create an accurate radius and they give you a place to start the saw blade. Drill these holes first.

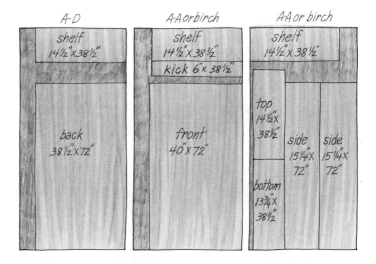

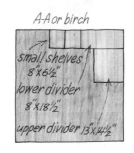

PLYWOOD LAYOUTS

56-2

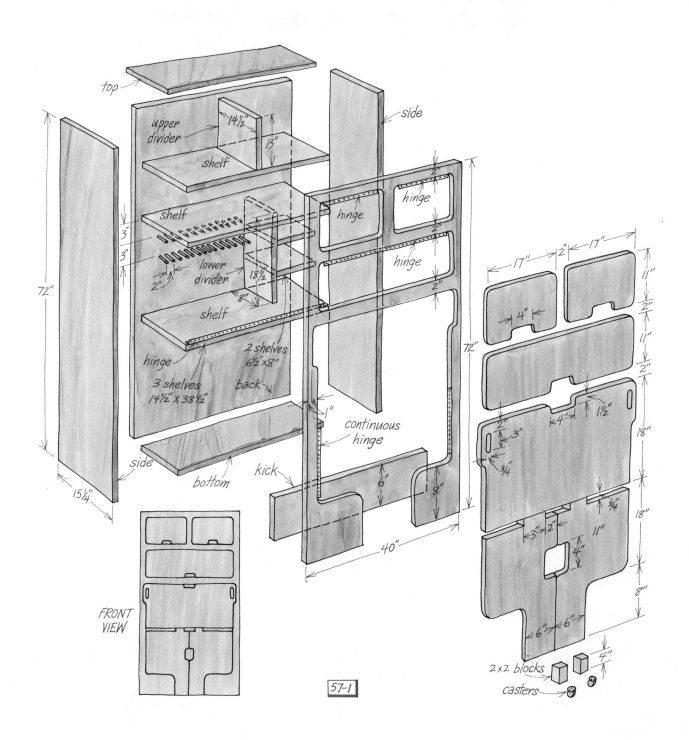

top

upper divider

14½"

13"

shelf

side

shelf

3"

3"

2"

lower divider

hinge

hinge

hinge

2"

72"

2"

18½"

8"

shelf

hinge

2 shelves 6½ x 8"

3 shelves 14½" X 38½"

back

continuous hinge

1"

72"

6"

8"

40"

15¼"

side

bottom

kick

FRONT VIEW

57-1

17"

2"

17"

11"

4"

2"

11"

2"

18"

2"

3"

4"

1½"

¾"

18"

3"

2"

11"

4"

¾"

4"

6"

6"

8"

2 x 2 blocks

casters

4"

Then carefully use the saber saw to cut out all the pieces. As you cut, check the blade frequently to be sure that the cut is perpendicular to the surface and not angled toward one side or the other. If you feel more comfortable using a handsaw, you can finish long, straight cuts with one.

Lay each door aside as you cut it out, but remember where it goes.

When you've cut them all out, glue and nail the face frame in place on the cabinet's front. Set the nails.

Sand any irregularities along the frame or door edges. Fill holes and voids in the plywood edges and sand lightly; repeat if necessary.

Drill all of the ¼" holes for the thread storage dowels, following the measurements given in drawing 57-1. Cut the dowels and glue them

into the holes.

Unless you wish to paint the hinges and casters, the best time to paint or finish the cabinet is before you put on the doors. Apply at least two coats of enamel or polyurethane.

Last, hinge the doors in place and screw the casters to short blocks on the door fronts as shown in drawing 57-1. Hinge placements are also shown in that drawing.

OUTDOOR FURNITURE

From plastic pipe, these pieces are durable, easy to make

Plastic pipe—technically called polyvinyl chloride or PVC—is an ideal material for making outdoor furniture. It's weatherproof, light-weight, and very easy to cut and assemble.

Shown in the photograph on the opposite page are four typical outdoor furniture pieces: a lounge, an easy chair, a footstool, and a small table. The instructions that follow will first give you information on working with plastic pipe. Refer to this section when making any of the pieces of furniture. Following that, under a separate heading for each project, you'll find the necessary tool and material lists, cutting schedules, and working drawings.

How to work with PVC pipe

To cut PVC pipe, you can use either a fine-toothed saw or a tube cutter equipped with a fine cutting wheel. After making a cut, remove burrs and bevel the cut end of the pipe slightly, using a knife. Before joining a pipe to an elbow, a tee, or any other fitting, sand the end of the pipe lightly where it will insert into the fitting.

Using a special solvent cement, you cement the pipe and fitting together. Methods of applying the solvent cement can vary. The normal method is to brush it liberally onto the pipe's end and lightly inside the fitting. Then push the two together and give the fitting a quarter turn to spread the solvent cement evenly. The cement sets up in about 15 seconds but takes an hour or so to cure.

To remove lettering and marks from surfaces of PVC, use lacquer thinner.

Footstool

Photo on facing page

This handy footstool adds to the easy chair's comfort or, used by itself, makes a comfortable perch for casual sitting.

TOOLS YOU'LL NEED: pencil · measuring tape · fine-toothed saw or tube cutter equipped with fine cutting wheel · knife · drill · ½" bit · grommet kit · fine sandpaper · sewing equipment.

MATERIALS LIST:

10' of 1½"-diameter PVC pipe
8 elbows, 90°, 1½"
2 lengths of ½"-diameter aluminum tubing, 22"
3 yards of 31"-wide synthetic chair canvas

Matching thread
Cord for lacing
Packet of grommets
4 pounds of shredded foam
4 upholstery buttons
4 buttons, ¾"
Lacquer thinner

HERE'S HOW

Cut and assemble the frame. Refer to the description in "How to work with PVC pipe" and to drawing 58-1. Here is the pipe cutting list, keyed to drawing 58-1:
   (A) Two pieces, 17⅝"
   (B) Four pieces, 6½"
   (C) Two pieces, 22⅜"
   Drill ½" holes for the aluminum tubing where specified; be sure to insert the tubing during assembly.

See page 76 for information on making cushions and slings. This footstool has a 15⅝" by 42" sling, laced to the pipe frame through grommets at the sling's ends. A simple 23" by 26" by 4" knife-edge cushion, stuffed with shredded foam, sits on top.

Drawing 25-3 on page 25 shows how to install upholstery buttons.

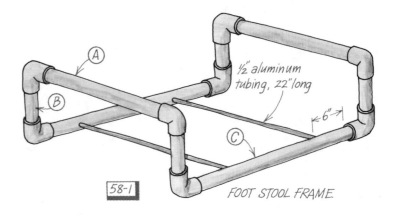

58-1

½" aluminum tubing, 22" long

6"

FOOT STOOL FRAME

Outdoor Furniture from Plastic Pipe   *Design: R. M. Eschen, Fitting Furniture*

Small Table

Photo above

The top of this small table is an inexpensive sink cutout (the part of a kitchen counter top that is removed for installation of a sink). For a small price, you should be able to buy one of these from a cabinetmaker, who can also square off the corners and band the edges with a plastic laminate that matches the top surface.

TOOLS YOU'LL NEED: pencil · measuring tape · fine-toothed saw or tube cutter equipped with fine cutting wheel · knife · drill · ³⁄₁₆″ bit · screwdriver · fine sandpaper.

MATERIALS LIST:
10' of 1½″-diameter PVC pipe
8 elbows, 90°, 1½″
1 sink cutout, about 21″ by 31″
4 round-head screws, 3″ by #10
Lacquer thinner

HERE'S HOW

Following the directions under "How to work with PVC pipe," page 58, cut and assemble the frame. Refer to drawing 59-1. Here are the lengths of the keyed parts:

(A) Two pieces, 22″
(B) Four pieces, 10″
(C) Two pieces, 13¼″

Drill ³⁄₁₆″ holes through (A) pieces for the screws that attach the top. Punch small starting holes for those screws in the underside of the top at matching locations, and screw the top in place.

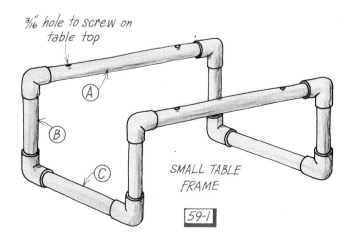

³⁄₁₆″ hole to screw on table top

SMALL TABLE FRAME

59-1

Easy Chair

Also see photo, page 59

Here is an easy chair that is durable enough to brave the elements, yet handsome enough for indoor use.

TOOLS YOU'LL NEED: pencil · measuring tape · fine-toothed saw or tube cutter equipped with fine cutting wheel · knife · drill · ½" bit · grommet kit · fine sandpaper · sewing equipment.

MATERIALS LIST:

23' of 1½"-diameter PVC pipe
8 elbows, 90°, 1½"
8 elbows, 45°, 1½"
6 tees, 1½"
5½ yards of 29"-wide synthetic chair canvas
Matching thread
Cord for lacing
Package of grommets
7 pounds of shredded foam
6 upholstery buttons
6 regular buttons, ¾"
Lacquer thinner

HERE'S HOW

Cut and assemble the frame pieces, following the directions under "How to work with PVC pipe" on page 58. Also refer to drawing 60-1 and the following cutting list.

    (A) Two pieces, 17¾"
    (B) Eight pieces, 2½"
    (C) Ten pieces, 6½"
    (D) Two pieces, 17"
    (E) Two pieces, 22"
    (F) One piece, 22⅝"

For information about making slings and cushions, see page 76. Make the seat sling a finished size of 15¾" by 74". Install grommets along the short ends, stitch it across the fold, and lace it as shown in drawing 61-1.

The back cushion is a 19" by 24" by 4" knife-edge cushion; the seat cushion is 21" by 24" by 4". Both are stuffed with shredded foam.

Add upholstery buttons as shown in drawing 25-3 on page 25. Put two in the back cushion and four in the seat cushion.

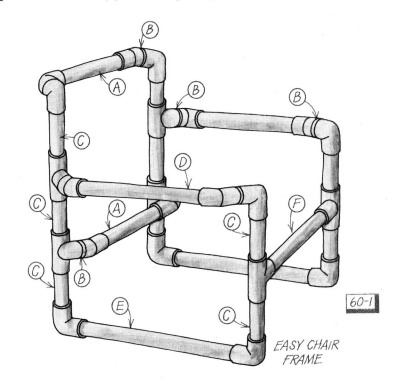

Easy Chair   *Plastic pipe chair is lightweight, comfortable.*

60-1

EASY CHAIR FRAME

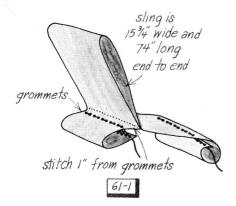

sling is 15¾" wide and 74" long end to end

grommets

stitch 1" from grommets

61-1

MATERIALS LIST:

46' of 1½"-diameter PVC pipe
10 tees, 1½"
14 elbows, 90°, 1½"
1 length of ½" aluminum tubing, 28"
2 carriage bolts, ½" by 5"
4 washers and nuts, ½"
7 yards of 31"-wide synthetic chair
   canvas
Matching thread
Cord for lacing
Packet of grommets
4 pounds of shredded foam
4 upholstery buttons
4 buttons, ¾"
Lacquer thinner

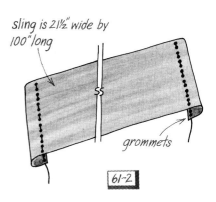

sling is 21½" wide by 100" long

grommets

61-2

Sun Lounge

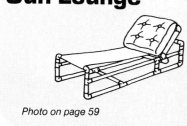

Photo on page 59

Because it is lightweight, this plastic-pipe sun lounge is easy to move in or out of the sun. In addition, it's comfortable, durable, and easy to make.

TOOLS YOU'LL NEED: pencil · measuring tape · fine-toothed saw or tube cutter equipped with fine cutting wheel · knife · drill · ½" bit · adjustable wrench · grommet kit · fine sandpaper · sewing equipment.

HERE'S HOW

Following the information given under "How to work with PVC pipe" on page 58, cut and assemble the frame pieces. Refer to drawing 61-3 and to the following cutting list.

(A) Seven pieces, 23½"
(B) Six pieces, 6⅜"
(C) Two pieces, 2½"
(D) Four pieces, 25½"
(E) Two pieces, 53½"
(F) Four pieces, 3½"
(G) Two pieces, 28"
(H) Two pieces, 22¼"

For information on making cushions and slings, see page 76. The main sling's finished length is 100" by 21½". Install grommets along the short ends and lace the sling to the frame as shown in drawing 61-2.

Make the backrest sling as shown in drawing 61-4. Slide it over the backrest.

The backrest cushion is a 30" by 26" knife-edge cushion. You can make it by following the instructions given on page 78. If you wish, you can also make a cushion to set on top of the main sling.

Add upholstery buttons as shown in drawing 25-3 on page 25.

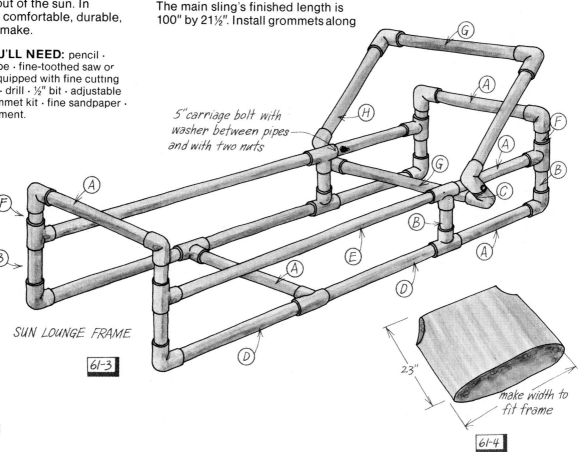

5" carriage bolt with washer between pipes and with two nuts

SUN LOUNGE FRAME

61-3

23"

make width to fit frame

61-4

Careful marking and cutting *along a guide ensure precise work. Versatile saber saw is one of the most useful cutting tools.*

TOOLS & TECHNIQUES

This section is meant to be a reference for you. If you're in doubt about any techniques necessary for making this book's projects, turn to these pages for help.

First comes a section on proportioning furniture for maximum comfort and efficiency. Next, a primer on materials will simplify buying lumber. Then woodworking information begins—how to measure and mark, cut, drill, assemble, and finish wood. Here you will learn how to cut cleanly, drill straight, drive screws, make simple joints, and much more. Ending the book is a section on working with foam and fabrics.

Sizing furniture for comfort

Furniture should make life easier. That's why it exists. Chairs provide a comfortable way to put ourselves in efficient positions for working or eating. Beds offer padded, level, warm sleeping spaces that are easy to get into and out of. Storage systems transform small amounts of floor space into large quantities of storage space. The list goes on and on.

The dimensions of a piece of furniture determine whether or not it will be efficient, comfortable, or even useful to us. A chair that is too tall is not comfortable to sit on. If a bed is too short, our feet get cold.

So, to avoid cold feet and other hazards, "human engineers" have compiled reams of statistics meant to make furniture comfortable and efficient.

Of course, comfort is relative to bodies. The only dimensions we can give in a limited amount of space are for "average" people. And most of us aren't average in size or in any other way. We are male, female, tall, short, thin, fat, young, old—and with scores of other differences. And even if two people are roughly the same height and weight, their proportions may differ. For example, the distance from knees to ankles may vary as much as 6 inches.

The drawings below and on page 64 show "average" dimensions for furniture. You can use these as a basis, but be sure to measure the people who will actually be using the furniture and revise the dimensions accordingly.

(Continued on page 64)

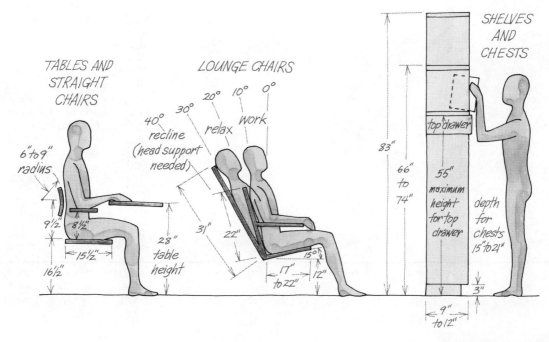

. . . Continued from page 63

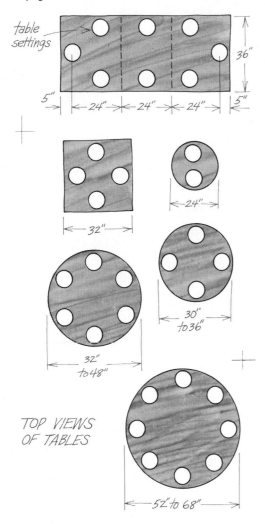

table settings

36"

5" — 24" — 24" — 24" — 5"

32"

24"

30" to 36"

32" to 48"

TOP VIEWS OF TABLES

52" to 68"

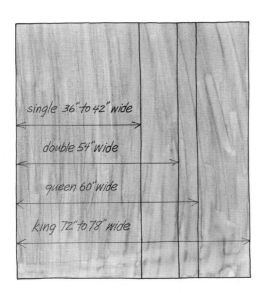

single 36" to 42" wide

double 54" wide

queen 60" wide

king 72" to 78" wide

BEDS (top view)

heights are generally 17" to 18" but go as high as 24"

Basics for buying lumber

You're standing at the lumberyard's checkout counter. The cash register's numbers spin madly like cherries in a slot machine. You wait with bated breath. Then it happens—the total slams into view. You lose.

It's tough to win, but the surest way to hedge your losses is to brief yourself before visiting the lumberyard. Know what to look for—lumber types, sizes, and grades—and know how they are sold. Judge your requirements carefully so you don't buy excessive amounts, inappropriate materials, or unnecessary quality. And, most important, shop around. Make a list of your requirements and call several dealers for the best price.

To help you prepare for your lumberyard experience, here is a basic lumber-buying primer.

Hardwood or softwood?

Wood is of two main types: hardwood and softwood. Hardwoods come from deciduous trees, softwoods from conifers. Hardwoods are usually—but not always—harder than softwoods. One clear example is balsa. Though the softest of woods, it is classified a hardwood.

Standard lumber is softwood. What we call a "1 by 4" or "2 by 4" is usually pine or fir. These two commonly used softwoods are good choices for making certain furniture pieces.

Fir is harder and stronger than pine but not nearly as strong as birch, oak, or other hardwoods. Because pine is probably the softest wood used in furniture making, it is also the easiest to work with for those who don't have many tools. It cuts easily and resists splintering.

Though most hardwoods are more expensive and harder to work than softwoods, and though some must be specially ordered, they offer certain advantages. Most hardwoods are very strong, have handsome grain and coloring, and lend themselves to finely tooled joinery. In addition, they finish beautifully with more resistance to wear. Typically used hardwoods include oak, birch, ash, walnut, and teak. Of these, ash and birch cost the least, walnut and teak the most.

If you are considering using hardwoods, call several dealers in your area to find out what species are available and what their prices are.

Hardwoods are usually the best choice where appearance is important, but because they're more expensive, don't use them where you don't need them.

What quality?

Choose wood that is "kiln dried," straight, and flat. Stay away from wood that is bowed, twisted, split, or warped. And unless you want to choose knots for effect, avoid them. By selecting your lumber piece by piece, you can get better lumber for your money. Check out the lesser grades, working your way up until you find something suitable.

What size?

Before you buy any softwood, you should know that a 2 by 4 is not 2" by 4". Like all milled softwood lumber, a 2 by 4 is given this size designation before it shrinks in drying and is planed to size. A 2 by 4 is actually 1½" by 3½". Other nominal and actual sizes are shown in the chart below.

Standard Dimensions of Finished Lumber

SIZE TO ORDER	SURFACED (Actual Size)
1 x 2	¾" x 1½"
1 x 3	¾" x 2½"
1 x 4	¾" x 3½"
1 x 6	¾" x 5½"
1 x 8	¾" x 7¼"
1 x 10	¾" x 9¼"
1 x 12	¾" x 11¼"
2 x 3	1½" x 2½"
2 x 4	1½" x 3½"
2 x 6	1½" x 5½"
2 x 8	1½" x 7¼"
2 x 10	1½" x 9¼"
2 x 12	1½" x 11¼"

Thickness of 3" lumber is 2½" and of 4" lumber is 3½".

Hardwood lumber is normally sold in odd lengths and sizes by the lineal foot, board foot, or even by the pound. When you need hardwood for a particular project, specify the footage you need and ask the salesperson to sell you what is in stock that will fill your requirements with the least waste. Again, hand pick your lumber if possible.

In case you have to calculate board feet for ordering, here is the formula: thickness in inches times width in feet times length in feet equals the number of board feet. Use the nominal sizes, not the actual ones. A 1 by 6 ten feet long would be computed $1" \times \frac{6}{12}' \times 10' = 5$ board feet. Another way to figure it is $1" \times \frac{1}{2}' \times 10' = 5$ board feet.

What about plywood?

Plywood has several advantages over lumber: exceptional strength, high resistance to warp, availability in large sheets, and, in most cases, lower cost.

Though you'll have a hard time finding lumber wider than 12", plywood comes in 4' by 8' sheets. These large sheets are excellent when you need large surfaces; for example, they eliminate the need for gluing several boards together to make a table top.

Plywood, like lumber, falls into two categories: softwood and hardwood. In the case of plywood, the difference lies in the species of wood used for the outer faces of a panel.

Birch-veneered plywood is a good selection in the hardwood category. Handsome, light-toned, and durable, it is one of the lowest-priced hardwood plywoods. Ash is another good low-cost choice. More expensive hardwood veneers include oak, walnut, and teak.

Plywood comes in a range of thicknesses: ⅛", ³⁄₁₆", ¼", ⅜", ½", ⅝", ¾". The thicker a sheet is, the more it costs, so you can save money by choosing the proper thickness.

In addition to hardwood-veneered panels, you can get softwood panels that are "resin-overlaid" or "density-overlaid." This means that the plywood has a resin-impregnated paper permanently fused to its surfaces. Medium-density panels are excellent for painting; high-density panels are attractive even when left unfinished.

A word about plywood edges: when filled, sanded, and finished

naturally, they can give a pleasing "butcher block" laminated appearance. But if you'd rather not see the edges, mask them with veneer tape or moldings. Several alternatives are shown below. You can also fill plain edges or cover them with veneer tape, then paint them.

Veneer tape is available in several widths and wood types, with or without adhesive backing. To apply the nonadhesive type, coat both the plywood edge and the back of the veneer tape with contact cement. Let the glue dry. Then, aligning one edge of the tape with an edge of the plywood, carefully lay the tape in place. Press it down firmly, then remove the excess tape with a razor blade or with sandpaper.

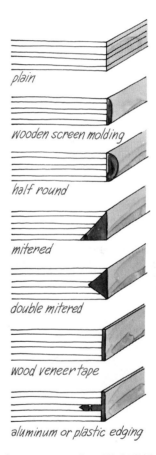

plain

wooden screen molding

half round

mitered

double mitered

wood veneer tape

aluminum or plastic edging

PLYWOOD EDGE TREATMENTS

How to measure and mark

Most important in starting a project properly are careful measuring and marking. These first woodworking steps will set the stage for your finished project. By precise measuring and marking, you can avoid wasting time and materials and take the first step toward professional-looking results.

For most projects, you'll use a pencil, a measuring tape, and a combination square. For some projects, you'll also need a yardstick and a compass.

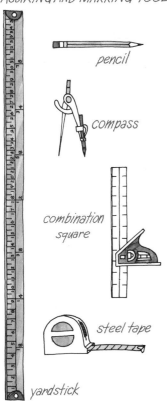

MEASURING AND MARKING TOOLS

pencil

compass

combination square

steel tape

yardstick

Measuring. Tight-fitting joinery requires measuring and cutting to within 1/32" or 1/64"; use a metal yardstick, tape measure, or the blade of a square. A tape measure's end hook should be riveted loosely so that it slides the distance of its

end hook adjusts for inside and outside measurements

own thickness, adjusting that thickness for precise "inside" and "outside" measurements.

Because measuring is easy and most materials are expensive, it pays to double-check your measurements. And whenever possible during construction, transfer measurements directly from one material to another rather than measuring again.

use one material to transfer measurements to another

Marking lines. A sharp pencil works well for drawing lines. Draw straight lines by guiding the pencil along the edge of a square or straightedge. Use a compass to draw curves or small circles.

For drawing large circles—such as the top for a round table—tack one end of a yardstick to the

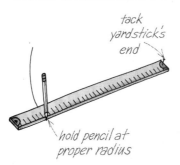

tack yardstick's end

hold pencil at proper radius

material's center and, holding the pencil at the proper radius, turn the yardstick like a large clock hand.

For marking straight across a board at 90° or at 45°, use a combination square.

Checking for square. Use a combination square for this purpose. Depending upon which side of the square's handle you use, you can check for a true 90° or 45° angle.

Place the handle of the square firmly along one of the board's side surfaces, sliding the blade into contact with the board end. If light shows between the blade and the board, the end is not true. Check across both the width and the thickness of the board. Plane or sand the dark ridges until the edge is square and no light shows through.

checking board's end for square

checking 45° miter

checking inside for square

Cutting wood

In furniture making, your cuts must be precise. They should be clean, square, and straight (unless they're supposed to be curved). When you join two pieces, no gaps should show between them.

For proper cutting, you need the right tools. What are the "right tools"? That depends upon the project.

Cutting tools range from the simple and inexpensive to the sophisticated and costly. Generally speaking, hand tools are considerably less expensive than power tools. But some power tools—such as saber saws and electric drills—come in inexpensive models that cost little more than their hand-powered counterparts.

Because a saber saw greatly simplifies both straight and curve cutting in materials as thick as 1 inch, it is an excellent tool for making many of the projects in this book.

Some projects require sophisticated tools, but there may be ways of getting around buying them. Following are three alternatives.

• You can have cuts made at the lumberyard. Most lumberyards make straight cuts for a small fee. If you decide to do this, have the yard make the longest cuts. But before you do, find out how much the cutting costs and whether or not it can be done precisely.

• You can join an adult education woodworking class. In many localities, high schools and colleges offer night classes on woodworking. These schools usually have excellent tools and very helpful instructors.

• One other alternative is to look up "Cabinet Makers" in the Yellow Pages and call two or three for cost estimates on doing procedures you are not equipped for. You'll probably have to take your plans in to get firm estimates.

Miscellaneous cutting tools. Though they don't fit the category of saws, tools such as chisels, planes, files, and the router are designed for cutting.

Chisels are used primarily for notching and cutting grooves (see "How to cut grooves" on page 68). They come in several sizes.

Planes slice off unwanted portions of wood, controlling the width and depth of their cut. A block plane—the short one—cuts end grain well. A jack plane, about twice the length of a block plane, shears bumps and irregularities off a board's edges.

Abrasive tools, such as files and rasps, remove small quantities of wood and make small areas smooth. They come in many shapes, sizes, and degrees of coarseness.

A router is versatile—it grooves, shaves, bevels, and rounds wood, depending upon the bit. This power

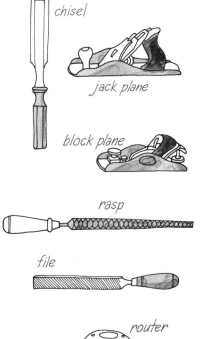

chisel

jack plane

block plane

rasp

file

router

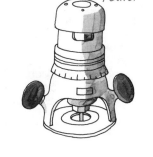

tool cuts straight grooves, V-shaped grooves, rounded grooves, and even exact dovetails. It can round or bevel the edge of a board in a single pass. Though rather expensive, a router can give projects a very finished look.

How to make a clean cut. The number of teeth per inch along a saw blade determines the kind of cut it makes. The more numerous the teeth, the smoother the cut. Choose a blade with 10 to 12 teeth per inch. For cutting plywood smoothly with power saws, various kinds of blades are made.

Wood tends to splinter and break away where saw teeth exit. The kind of saw you use will determine the side of the wood on which this happens. Some saws have upward-cutting blades; others cut downward. If you're not sure, look to see which direction the teeth point.

Cut with the good side up when using a handsaw, table saw, or radial-arm saw. If you use a portable circular saw or saber saw, cut the wood good-side-down. To minimize splintering, score along the backside of the cutting line. Or try taping the line's backside with masking tape. Better yet, back the cut by pressing a scrap next to the piece you're cutting and cut both pieces together.

Don't forget to support both halves of the piece you're cutting. Otherwise the saw will bind and, as you near the end of the cut, the unsupported piece will break away. If the saw binds anyway, stick a screwdriver blade in the end of the cut to spread it open.

Sawing straight lines. Several kinds of saws can cut straight lines: handsaw, saber saw, power circular saw, table saw, and radial-arm saw. The right method for cutting straight depends upon the saw you use.

The secret of cutting straight is using a guide. Table saws and radial-arm saws have built-in guides, but if you use a hand-held saw, you'll have to improvise a guide or use a small guide attachment.

(Continued on page 68)

. . . Continued from page 67

Guide a handsaw against a board clamped along the cutting line. Start a cut by drawing the saw slowly *up* a few times to make a notch or "kerf." Then saw with short

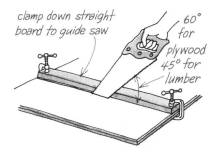

clamp down straight board to guide saw

60° for plywood 45° for lumber

strokes at the blade's wide end, progressing to smooth, long, generous strokes. Keep your forearm in line with the blade as you work. Saw lumber at a 45° angle; cut plywood and other sheet materials at 60°.

Making a full kerf about ½" into the board's far edge will help to guide the blade straight for the rest of the cut.

Saber saws usually come with a guide designed for making straight cuts a short distance from, and parallel to, a board's edge. When cutting across panels or wide surfaces, guide the saw's base plate against a straightedge clamped a measured distance from the cutting line. Keep the saw firmly against the guide and check the blade continually to see that it doesn't bend away from the cut; it should stay vertically straight. Wear eye protection when using a saber saw.

Power circular saws also come with guides for ripping narrow widths. For cutting large panels, make a reusable guide from scrap plywood and molding as shown below. Work carefully and wear eye protection.

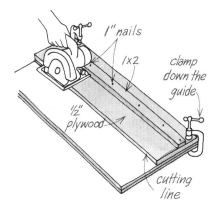

1" nails

1x2

clamp down the guide

½" plywood

cutting line

Sawing curves and irregular lines. Blades for sawing curves, zigzags, or irregular cuts must be thin and narrow. They are used in an almost straight up-and-down position. Saws suitable for this kind of cutting are the keyhole saw, coping saw, and saber saw.

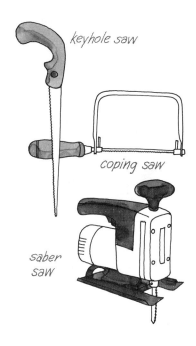

keyhole saw

coping saw

saber saw

The keyhole saw is the hand-powered version of the saber saw. With it you can cut curves and make cutouts in the center of panels, but you must start it from a drilled hole.

The coping saw, limited by its metal frame, cuts tightly curved lines close to a board's edge. Its blade is removable. When cutting vertically in a vise, point the teeth toward the handle and cut on the pull stroke. When working on something supported horizontally, point the teeth away from the handle and cut on the push stroke.

The saber saw can do almost any kind of cutting. A great general purpose tool, it tracks curved lines easily. For greatest control, get a saber saw with a variable-speed trigger.

How to make a cutout. Using a saber saw, you can dip into a panel's center to make a cutout by tilting the saw forward on its toe plate, starting the motor, and slowly lowering the tool. Do this with care, wearing eye protection.

You can also make a cutout by drilling a hole about 1" in diameter, then using this hole to start a cut with a keyhole saw. Once you have cut a few inches, you can finish a long cut with a regular handsaw.

How to cut a miter. A miter is simply a through cut made at an angle—usually 45.° Mark the miter first, using a combination square; then cut it just as you would cut straight across the board, but holding the saw at a slightly flatter angle. Use a fine-toothed saw and cut to the outside of the cutting line.

A great aid for cutting miters is a miter box. It supports small material securely and guides the saw for precise cuts.

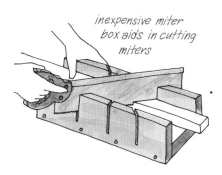

inexpensive miter box aids in cutting miters

Radial-arm saws and table saws are excellent for cutting precise miters.

How to cut grooves. Grooves are probably the most difficult kind of cuts to make, especially using hand tools. The trick is to cut a wide groove with a flat base.

Power tools cut grooves easily. The best tools are routers and power saws equipped with dado blades. You simply guide them across the surface—the bits or blades do all the work. Or, using a power saw with a regular blade, you can make a series of joined cuts within the area to be removed. You can also get an inexpensive attachment for a power drill to cut grooves to about 1" deep; check your hardware store.

To cut a groove using hand tools, first mark the groove; then saw to the inside of the lines as deep as you want the groove. If it's a very wide cut, saw several extra cuts across the waste wood in the middle. Then use a chisel to remove the waste wood.

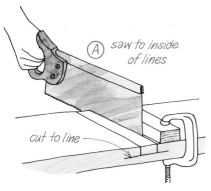

(A) saw to inside of lines

cut to line

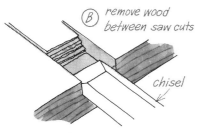

(B) remove wood between saw cuts

chisel

If the groove doesn't extend to the board's edges, cut it with a chisel. Rap the chisel lightly on each across-grain mark (with the

CUTTING A SHALLOW GROOVE, USING A CHISEL

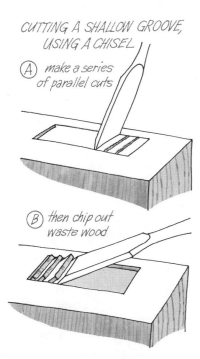

(A) make a series of parallel cuts

(B) then chip out waste wood

bevel facing waste wood) to keep the wood from splitting beyond those marks. Then make a series of parallel cuts to the desired depth, moving with the blade's bevel forward. Keep the chisel almost vertical to the surface.

Next, using the chisel without the hammer and decreasing its angle considerably, chip out all the waste wood. Make final smoothing cuts with the chisel's bevel almost flat against the wood.

For a deep groove, remove excess wood first by drilling a series of holes. Then join the holes and square up the resulting mortise with a chisel.

MAKING A DEEP GROOVE

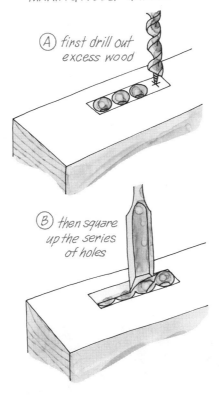

(A) first drill out excess wood

(B) then square up the series of holes

How to cut slots. Several of this book's projects consist of panels joined by interlocking joints. In the joinery section of this book, on page 74, you'll learn how to make an interlocking joint. Such a joint requires that you cut a slot in both panels. Cutting this kind of slot is a simple job if you know how.

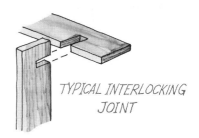

TYPICAL INTERLOCKING JOINT

Here's how:

Mark for the cuts as described in the joinery section, using a square. When you cut, be sure to cut to the *waste* side of the cutting lines. Remember, too, that it's better to remove too little wood than too much—you can always take off a little more, but adding wood is another story.

One way to cut a slot is to begin by drilling a hole the same diameter as the slot's width, located at the end of the slot. Then cut from the panel's

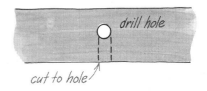

drill hole

cut to hole

edge to the hole. If necessary, square off the rounded end, using a saber saw, keyhole saw, or file.

You can also cut a slot with a saber saw or a coping saw, as shown below. This is the easiest method.

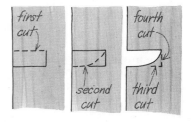

first cut

second cut

third cut

fourth cut

If you don't have a saber saw or a coping saw, you can cut a slot with a handsaw and chisel, as described under the heading "How to cut grooves," facing page.

Drilling straight, clean holes

For many of this book's projects, you'll need a drill. Though hand drills can do most of the work, a ¼" or ⅜" power drill is highly recommended. For one thing, it makes the job of drilling much faster and easier; for another, with an abundance of available attachments, it can become one of the most useful tools in your tool box.

Four drilling problems crop up often: 1) Centering the moving drill bit on its mark; 2) Drilling a hole straight; 3) Keeping the wood's backside from breaking away as the drill bit pierces; and 4) Drilling to a measured depth and knowing when to stop. The following techniques will help rid your work of these problems.

For information on drilling pilot holes and countersinking, see "How to drive screws," page 72.

How to center the bit. Keep a pointed tool handy for center punching. A couple of taps with a hammer on a large nail, nailset, or punch will leave a hole to prevent the bit from wandering.

punch a hole to keep drill bit from wandering

How to drill straight. A drill press or a press accessory for your hand drill offers the best means for drilling holes straight. But if you don't have one of these, try one of

drill guide

block

align with square

the three methods shown above. You can use a commercially available drill guide for twist bits, make a guide by predrilling a scrap block of wood, or use a square to align the drill visually.

How to drill cleanly. To keep a drill bit from breaking out through the backside of the wood, do one of two things: 1) Lay or clamp a wood scrap

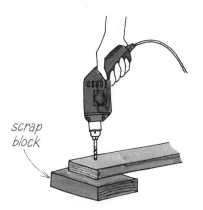

scrap block

firmly against the backside of your workpiece and drill through the workpiece into the scrap; or 2) Just after the drill's point pierces, flop the workpiece over and finish drilling from the other side.

How to gauge depth. To stop a drill bit at the right depth, wrap a piece of tape around the shank to signal the proper boring depth.

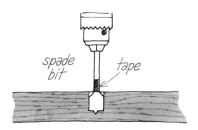

spade bit   tape

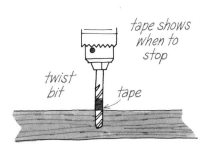

tape shows when to stop

twist bit   tape

General drilling tips. Clamp materials down, particularly when using a power drill. The torque can easily wrench the wood from your grasp, especially when you're using a large bit. Hold the drill firmly, leaving the motor on until you have withdrawn the bit from the wood. To avoid breaking small bits, don't tilt the drill once the bit has entered the wood. Wear plastic safety goggles, especially when your workpiece has a brittle surface.

Fastening and joinery techniques

After you have marked, cut, and drilled pieces, the next logical step is joinery—fastening the pieces together to form a finished project. Though wood can be cut to form dozens of kinds of joints, the methods of fastening those joints are few: gluing and clamping, nailing, screwing, and bolting. This section tells how to use fasteners and how to make basic joints.

Basic fastening tools are shown at right. They are all relatively inexpensive hand tools. Of course, a saw is needed for cutting most types of joints; saws are discussed on page 67 under "Cutting wood."

Gluing and clamping. One of the best fasteners for permanent joints is glue. Glue strengthens almost all joints. Unless you use contact cement or epoxy (depending upon what you are gluing), you should clamp the joint after applying glue. C-clamps, bar clamps, or pipe clamps will handle most standard clamping jobs.

Most projects in this book specify white glue. It has moderate moisture resistance and strength; it works well on wood and is easy to use. Spread it on the adjoining surfaces, clamp them tightly together, wipe off the excess, and let dry according to label recommendations. Be sure to wipe off the excess—most stains and transparent finishes will not take to glue-coated areas.

Choose and use other kinds of glue according to their labels.

C-clamps work well for miscellaneous clamping jobs. They come in various sizes, with openings from 3" to 16". Protect wooden surfaces from damage from a metal clamp's jaws by slipping a scrap block between the jaws and the wood before you tighten the clamp.

Bar clamps and pipe clamps work well for clamping across broad surfaces. Bar clamps open as far as the bar part of the clamp allows. Pipe clamps depend for their maximum spread upon the length of pipe you attach them to.

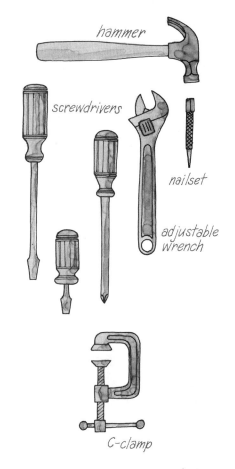

hammer

screwdrivers

nailset

adjustable wrench

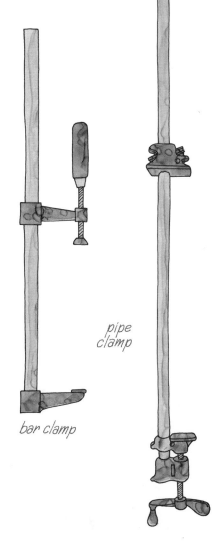

pipe clamp

C-clamp

bar clamp

How to nail. Nailing is easy, inexpensive, and fast. It works fine where only medium strength is needed—but use glue too. Never expect nails to hold a chair's primary joints or other joints where they might work loose.

Nails with sharp points hold better than blunt ones, but they tend to split wood. Before driving a nail into wood that splits easily,

don't line up nails along same grain line

no   *yes*

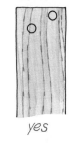

blunt the point with a tap of the hammer. And don't line up two nails along the same grain lines in the board—the wood will probably split if you do. Instead, stagger nails slightly.

When starting a nail, hold it near its head. That way, if you miss, you'll only knock your fingers away. Once the nail is started, let go of it and swing the hammer with fuller strokes, hitting the nail's head squarely. Visualize a pivot point

keep pivot point level with nail head

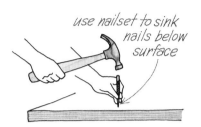

use nailset to sink nails below surface

How to drive screws. Though screws are slightly more difficult and time-consuming to drive than nails, they are considerably stronger, especially when supplemented with glue. Screws used without glue can be removed, creating a joint that can be taken apart.

Drill pilot holes for screws. Either select a drill bit slightly smaller than the screw's shank or use a "pilot bit." As shown in the drawing below,

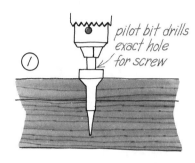

pilot bit drills exact hole for screw

① ② ③

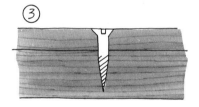

insert a dowel when screwing into end grain

at the handle's end and keep that point level with the nail head.

Where you are concerned about the wood's appearance, be very careful not to crush the surface with the last few hammer blows; use a nailset to set the nail heads below the surface about 1/16". Then fill the holes with putty.

When pulling a nail, put a scrap block under the hammer's head so you won't damage the surface of the wood.

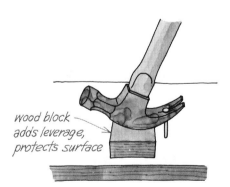

wood block adds leverage, protects surface

this bit drills a hole that's just the right shape for a particular screw. Some bits are adjustable; others match a particular screw size. The latter type is the more reliable.

When screwing into end grain, it's a good idea first to drill a hole and insert a hardwood dowel. This gives

the screw something strong to grip.

Be sure to use a screwdriver that fits the screw's slot, not one that's too small or too large. And don't work with a burred or bent screwdriver.

If you don't want screw heads to show, countersink them below the wood's surface; then fill the hole above the head with putty or with a wooden plug. To use a wooden plug, drill the countersinking hole from 1/8" to 3/8" deep and, instead of doweling, use a "plug-cutter" bit to cut the plug from a scrap of the same wood. This way, the grain and color of the plug will match that of the wood you're plugging.

How to use bolts. Unlike a screw, which digs into wood, a bolt has a threaded shaft that grips a nut. Because it grips the nut rather than the wood, a bolt is very strong and doesn't chew up the wood when removed.

Several types of bolts are available, with varying kinds of heads. Some you tighten with a screwdriver,

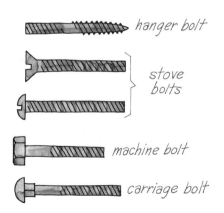

hanger bolt

stove bolts

machine bolt

carriage bolt

others with a wrench. You drive a hanger bolt by running two nuts on the shaft, tightening them together, and then driving the top nut with a wrench.

You can countersink a bolt head the same way you'd countersink a screw (see "How to drive screws," facing page). But if you want the bolts to be removable, carriage bolts are the only kind you can plug or fill over; with others, you wouldn't be able to get the proper tool on the bolt's head.

Several kinds of nuts are available. The kinds most used for this book's projects are hex nuts, acorn nuts, wing nuts, and T-nuts. T-nuts fit flush

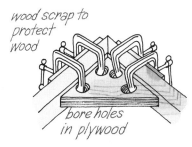

on a surface and provide metal threads in a hole. A T-nut is strong only when pulled from the side of the hole opposite its body—it can't withstand a pull from the same side.

How to make a butt joint. Measure the pieces and mark them with a 90° square. Cut them carefully so they won't show gaps. Add glue and clamps and/or fasteners such as screws, nails, or dowels.

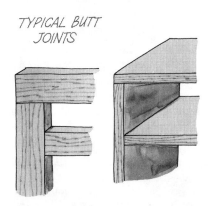

TYPICAL BUTT JOINTS

How to make a miter joint. Measure the pieces, remembering that both must go the full distance to the corner. Mark them, using a 45°

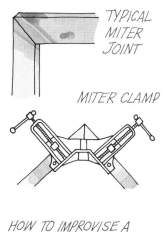

TYPICAL MITER JOINT

MITER CLAMP

HOW TO IMPROVISE A MITER CLAMP

wood scrap to protect wood

bore holes in plywood

angle, and cut carefully. Apply glue to the two joining surfaces and clamp, using a special clamp made for this purpose or improvising one as shown above. Add fasteners for strength.

How to make a dowel joint. You'll encounter two different kinds of dowel joints; one is quite easy to make, but the other is more difficult, requiring special tools and careful drilling.

The first type involves cutting a basic butt joint, joining the two pieces by holding or clamping them together, and drilling holes *through* one and into the other. Next, you score small grooves along the dowels so glue can escape the holes. Then you coat the dowels and the two meeting surfaces with glue, and pound the dowels in from the outside.

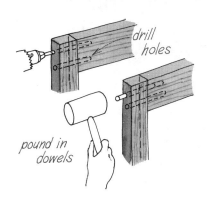

drill holes

pound in dowels

The other method, perhaps more common, is blind doweling. With this method, the dowels don't show. Instead, you mark and drill separate,

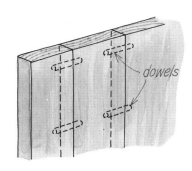

dowels

matching holes in the two meeting halves, add glue, push dowels into one of the halves, and then fit the two halves together.

doweling jig aids in drilling dowel holes

The tough part is getting the holes to match exactly and drilling them straight (see page 70). A tool called a "doweling jig" is made especially for this purpose. Clamp this tool onto one of the surfaces and drill through the guide holes. Then clamp the adjoining surface in place, unclamp the first piece, and

hex nut   square nut

wing nut   T-nut

acorn ("cap") nut

drill the matching holes in the second surface.

Or you can mark the two pieces as shown below. Do your best to drill the holes straight (see page 70).

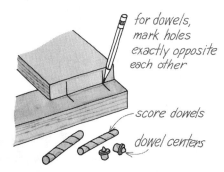

for dowels, mark holes exactly opposite each other

score dowels

dowel centers

You can also use "dowel centers." To do this, drill the holes in one surface, put the centers in the holes, and push the other piece in place against the first one. The dowel centers mark the exact place to drill.

Before pounding in dowels, cut them slightly shorter than the combined depth of the matching holes. Then score them and spread glue along them. Insert the dowels, put the two halves together, and clamp the joint tight.

How to make a spline joint. Inserting a wooden spline in a saw kerf is a simple way to strengthen miter and butt joints.

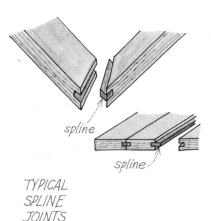

spline

spline

TYPICAL
SPLINE
JOINTS

To be sure the grooves match, use the same table saw or router setting to cut them. The width of the spline should be slightly less than the combined depth of the kerfs. For most work, a good spline size is ¼" thick by 1¼" wide. For this, you'd cut a groove ¼" wide and about $1\frac{1}{16}$" deep in each meeting piece.

Cut the spline, spread glue along it, and put it in place in one of the grooves. Then push the other half in place and clamp.

How to make an interlocking joint. The simple slide-together joints shown below are used for several of

INTERLOCKING JOINTS

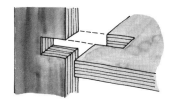

this book's projects. Flat interlocking joints between boards may require fasteners, but long-slot interlocking joints for plywood panels—those used in the wine rack on page 39, for example—work well without fasteners. And you can disassemble them simply by sliding them apart.

To make them, cut matching grooves in the two pieces. The width of each groove should be exactly the same as that of the connecting piece. Normally, the grooves' depths are figured to intersect midway between the two pieces.

Mark for the grooves, using the joining piece as a guide. Then cut the grooves as explained under "How to cut grooves" and "How to cut slots" on pages 68 and 69.

Finishing wood

Wood should be given a finish to protect it from being soiled, stained, or dented. A finish can also enhance the appearance of most woods. But before you apply a finish, prepare the wood by filling holes and imperfections and sanding it smooth.

Filling holes. Before filling wood, consider the finish you plan to apply. Don't use a filler that's going to stick out like a sore thumb. Of course, if you plan to paint the project, practically any filler will work—the paint should cover all.

For natural finishes, fill blemishes with wood dough or stick shellac (a specialty product for furniture makers). Both products come in colors that match most woods.

Spread wood dough with a putty knife; melt stick shellac into the hole or crack. Always build up the patch slightly above the surface and then sand off the excess. To patch a large hole, fill the hole, let the compound dry, sand the surface on and around the patch, and then repeat the process.

When you plan to stain the wood, you should use a slightly different treatment. Because dried fillers don't have the same porosity as woods, they often show up under stains—the stain gets absorbed unevenly. So choose a wood dough that is close to the wood's finished color and apply it *after* the stain.

You can touch up with stain if necessary, and then apply a finish coat of clear polyurethane. First test the color match on an extra piece of wood. You'll find that dark stains and opaque stains usually camouflage fillers best.

Whether you're applying a natural finish, staining, or painting, seal knots with shellac before finishing— this will prevent sap from seeping through.

Sanding wood. Though sanding is sometimes a tedious job, it can give your project a professional touch. So don't neglect it—after working hard at making a project, you shouldn't scrimp with the part that shows the most.

A power sander makes sanding easy, but unless you have a large

CHARACTERISTICS OF COMMON FINISHES

	Advantages	Disadvantages	General traits
CLEAR FINISHES			
Penetrating resin	Easiest of all finishes to apply. Gives wood a natural, no-finish look.	Provides little surface protection from heat, liquids, and abrasion.	Soaks into wood pores rather than coating the surface. Darkens wood grain.
Polyurethane varnish	Simple to apply by brush. Tough. Alcohol, heat, and water resistant.	Dries slowly. Sanding is required between coats. Can't be used over many other surface finishes.	Protects wood with thick surface coating. Enhances wood grain with slight darkening effect.
Shellac	Very fast drying. Easy to thin and apply. Very tough. Will not mar or scratch easily.	Alcohol, ammonia, and detergent dissolve it. Water will turn it white unless finish is waxed often.	Multiple coats lie on the wood surface and provide a slightly amber-tinted finish.
Lacquer	Primes, seals, and finishes all in one step. Very resistant to alcohol, chemicals, heat, abrasion.	Because it is extremely fast-drying, you must work quickly. Can be used only over bare wood or other lacquer.	Protects wood with thin layer of surface coating. Available for both spraying and brushing.
STAINS			
Pigmented oil stain	Simple to wipe on and off with a rag. Useful for making one wood species look like another in color.	Too pigmented to use on many fine furniture woods—often obscures pores and grain.	Colors are nonfading, non-bleeding, and available ready-mixed in a wide variety of hues.
Penetrating oil stain	Not pigmented, so pores and grain are revealed. Similar to a penetrating resin, only with color added.	Penetrates irregularly on softwoods and plywoods. Not good for making one wood look like another.	Soaks into wood rather than coating it. Colors by means of dyes rather than pigments.
Water stain	Colors are brilliant, warm-toned, clear, permanent. Stain thins easily and cleans up with water.	The wood fibers are swelled by the water, making light resanding necessary. Very slow drying and difficult to apply without experience.	Stain is available in powdered dye form that you mix with water. Wood fibers are colored by the dye in the same way that a piece of cloth is dyed.
Non-grain-raising (alcohol) stain	Cool-toned, transparent colors. Rapid drying may be useful if you have many projects to do. Good for use on hardwoods.	Very short drying time makes it difficult to use. Best when sprayed. Not for use on softwoods or plywoods.	Available in ready-mixed colors and in powdered form.
ENAMELS			
Oil-based enamel	Durable, washable, good adhesion, covers surface well.	Slow drying. Mineral spirits are required for thinning and cleanup.	Totally hides wood. All colors available in gloss, semi-gloss, and flat.
Latex enamel	Dries quickly. Thins and cleans up easily with water.	Less durability and coverage than oil-based enamels.	Totally hides wood. All colors available in semigloss and flat.

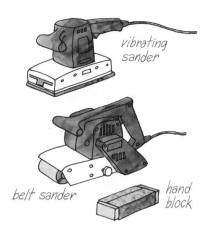

vibrating sander

belt sander   hand block

amount of sanding to do, you won't need one. Though hand sanding takes elbow grease, it produces a fine finish.

If you have one, a belt sander can remove a lot of wood fast. Use it only *in line* with the wood's grain. Graduate from coarse to fine sanding belts, but be careful—a belt sander with a coarse belt can devour your project.

Vibrating sanders work more like hand sanding. Some move the sandpaper in an "orbiting" motion; others move it back and forth. For final sanding use only the kind that works back and forth, and keep the movement in the same direction as the wood's grain.

Whether you sand by hand or power, divide the process into three steps: rough, preparatory (after you've filled defects), and finish. Rough-sand with 80-grit sandpaper; preparatory-sand with 120-grit; and finish-sand with 180-grit or finer. A final hand sanding usually improves the appearance of a finish. Prior to finishing, remove dust, using a rag moistened with mineral spirits.

Applying the finish. Many projects in this book recommend poly-urethane as a finish. Available both clear and pigmented, it is durable and easy to apply with a rag.

Three kinds of polyurethane are available: gloss, satin, and pene-trating sealer. Gloss and satin lie on the surface, giving it a plastic-coated appearance. Gloss, of course, is shinier than satin. Penetrating sealer soaks into the wood, protecting it from within. Choose this kind for maximum highlighting of wood texture.

Hundreds of varnishes, lacquers, oils, stains, enamels, and other finishes are available. Find out more about these from your dealer.

For a few of this book's projects, you'll need some basic know-how in working with fabrics and stuffings. Couches have cushions; some chairs have slings; and you'll even find a sling-hung cushion on the headboard on page 46. This section offers basic sewing information and shows how to stuff and stitch cushions.

How to stitch a finished edge. Where fabric will be seen from both sides—the sling on the back of a chair, for example—finish the edges so fraying won't show. To do this, first fold under ¼", then fold under another ¼", then pin. Stitch along the resulting triple thickness.

How to sew a loop. A small loop along a fabric edge is called a casing. With some projects you push a drawstring through this loop; in others, the loop holds a dowel or some other wooden frame member.

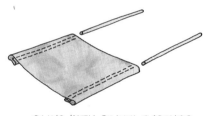

SLING WITH DOWEL CASINGS AT EACH END

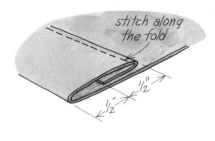

stitch along the fold

½" ½" ½"

DETAIL OF CASING FOR A DRAWSTRING

Make a casing by figuring the necessary loop size, plus ½", folding over the end to create the loop, tucking the unfinished fabric edge under about ½", and stitching along the fold. Choose heavy-duty thread and double-stitch for strength.

To make a large loop of fabric, join the two ends with a flat-fell seam. To do this, sew the two pieces together about ⅝" from their ends.

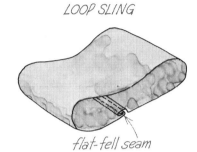

LOOP SLING

flat-fell seam

Press the joined ends down to one side; then trim the lower seam allowance to ¼". Curl the top seam allowance under it about ⅛" and pin. Topstitch it close to the fold; then turn it right side up and topstitch close to the seam for added strength.

Cushion stuffings

A cushion is generally a fabric bag filled with something soft—usually polyurethane foam or foam rubber. Some cushions have foam cores wrapped with one or more layers of polyester batting (a thick, fluffy fabric).

For each of the cushions described in this book's projects, we've recommended a particular stuffing. The various stuffings are discussed here; you can vary a stuffing, depending upon the appearance and comfort you want the cushion to have.

Foam blocks. Most firm, flat, squared-off cushions have one-piece or layered foam-block fillings. Foam blocks come in thicknesses of 1" increments. They are sold by the square foot. Price depends upon the size, the density, the amount of cutting necessary, and, most of all, the type of foam. There are two kinds: polyurethane foam ("polyfoam") and foam rubber.

Polyfoam is much cheaper than foam rubber but lacks durability, breaking down in sunlight and with use. Foam rubber weighs more. Both come in four densities: super-soft, soft, medium, and dense. Foam rubber tends to be firmer than polyfoam in the same classification: a "soft" foam rubber is usually about the same density as a "medium" polyfoam.

Most cushions are made up from two or more densities. A seat cushion, for example, commonly has a medium or dense foam core sandwiched by two outer layers (about 1" thick) of soft foam. A typical back cushion is made the same way, but its outer layers are of super-soft foam. Additionally, cushions with a soft, rounded look are usually wrapped with at least one layer of batting.

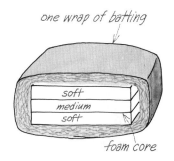

TYPICAL SEAT CUSHION STUFFING

Buy precut blocks at large yardage stores or upholstery supply shops. For custom sizes or styles, visit an upholstery shop or a foam dealer. To find foam dealers, look in the Yellow Pages under "Rubber— Foam & Sponge."

Working with foam is easy. Use a serrated bread knife or, even better, an electric carving knife to cut it. For maximum cutting ease, spray the knife's blade with silicone or a nonstick vegetable coating. To glue various foam pieces together, buy from a foam dealer easy-to-use foam adhesive made for the purpose.

Foam bolsters and pillows. Polyfoam and foam rubber also come in precut pillow forms and in cylindrical bolsters. Bolsters, specified for some of this book's projects, are sold by foam density and by diameter and length.

Shredded foam. The easiest form of cushion stuffing to obtain— shredded foam—is sold in yardage, notion, and variety stores. Basically, it is the same foam discussed under "Foam blocks," chopped into small chunks by a shredder. Shredded foam is cheap and easy to stuff into a fabric form; but those are practically its only virtues. It looks and feels lumpy, doesn't hold a particular shape, and is messy. If you plan to stuff a cushion with shredded foam, consider making an inner bag of muslin so you can remove the cover easily for cleaning.

Polyester batting. This synthetic has the feel of fluffy cotton. In cushion making, it's most commonly wrapped around foam blocks to soften and round them. For this purpose it's sold by the yard with a muslin backing. It is also sold in loose bulk form for stuffing cushions completely and in bed-size sheets for padding quilts.

Super-soft foam is best for the main softening of a cushion. Use the batting—at most two or three wraps—to round edges and give a cushion height. Batting settles with use; if you overwrap cushions, they may "deflate" in time.

To give cushion edges and corners a very round effect, trim the foam at an angle along the edges before you wrap. To soften all edges, wrap from front to back as well as from side to side.

Secure wrapped batting around foam by handstitching the loose end to the batting layer beneath it.

Choosing a fabric

When selecting an upholstery fabric, you may consider its appearance first of all. But this is not the only factor to think about. Here are a few other considerations:

Texture. Coarse fabrics snag clothing and are uncomfortable to sit on if you're wearing thin clothing. Slippery fabrics slide you away from back support. Choose fabrics that can breathe; if they can't, you'll perspire.

Textured fabrics with a nap— such as velvet, fake fur, and some types of suede cloth—must be sewn with all the nap going in one direction. Sometimes this means buying extra fabric.

Washability. Washable fabrics are generally more desirable than those that must be dry cleaned. Even better for maintenance are fabrics with spot-resistant finishes, soil-release finishes, and permanent-press finishes.

You should preshrink washable fabrics. Do this the same way you'll wash and dry the finished cover.

Patterned fabrics. Before you buy a print or striped fabric, visualize it on the completed project. If you choose a striped fabric, decide the direction of the stripes and determine whether you'll need extra fabric for matching the stripes. For patterned fabrics, plan to direct the pattern one way and decide whether or not you're going to match it. Compensate for this when you figure yardage.

Making cushions

A cushion isn't hard to define—it's just stuffing held by a fabric bag. The way you sew the bag together will make a difference in the cushion's shape. A discussion of the main types and how to make them follows.

A word about preparation: choose your method before buying the fabric—it can make a difference in the necessary amount.

Preshrink the fabric (if washable) and cut it out carefully.

In the construction, be sure to allow for an opening large enough to push the stuffing through. And decide how you'll close that opening. If you use a zipper, hook-and-pile tape, or upholstery tape with snaps, install the device according to manufacturer's directions while the cover is inside out.

KNIFE-EDGE CUSHION

Making knife-edge cushions. The drawing above shows an example of a knife-edge cushion. This style is quite easy to make, but it has a less definite shape than the box cushion discussed at right.

Here's how:

1) Cut the two fabric halves and put them face to face. If you plan to install a zipper, sew it to the pieces first, following the directions on the package.

2) Stitch the fabric together along three sides, about ½" in from the edges.

3) Trim off excess seam allowance and turn the cover right side out. Stuff the cover.

4) If you didn't put in a zipper, close the opening with an overcast stitch.

MAKING A KNIFE-EDGE CUSHION

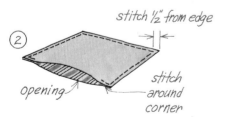

③ *turn right side out and stuff with foam*

④ *close opening with overcast stitch*

Making box cushions. These cushions have side panels that help maintain their rectangular shape. One is shown below. Box cushions are harder to make than knife-edge cushions.

BOX CUSHION

Here's how:

1) Cut out the six pieces, allowing for a ½" seam allowance around all edges. Plan an extra ⅝" for each side of a zipper.

2) Install a zipper in one of the side panels, or plan for a similar closure.

3) Working on the wrong side of the fabric, sew the four side panels together end to end, allowing about ½" seams.

4) Sew the side panels to the top and bottom panels. Trim excess allowances.

5) Turn the cover right side out and fill it.

MAKING A BOX CUSHION

① *six fabric pieces*

② *zipper OR closure*

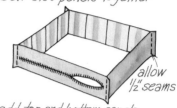

③ *sew side panels together*

allow ½" seams

④ *add top and bottom panels*

⑤ *turn right side out and stuff with foam*

Making drawstring covers. Bolsters (like those on the lounge chair on page 12) and other round-form cushions can be covered with drawstring covers. These are very easy to make.

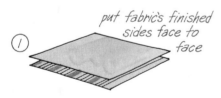

DRAWSTRING COVER

put fabric's finished sides face to face

stitch ½" from edge

opening

stitch around corner

Here's how:

1) Cut the fabric to fit the shape.

2) For a cover open only at one end, first make a knife-edge cushion cover, as described on page 78. For a cover open at both ends, seam the two ends of the fabric together, forming a cylinder that fits the cushion shape, and press the seam open.

3) Make the casings for the draw-strings at one end or both ends by folding the fabric's edge over twice and stitching along the first fold. Leave a ½" opening for the draw-string. (See the detail drawing under "How to sew a loop," page 76.)

4) Fasten a safety pin onto one end of the drawstring and fish it through the casing. Adjust the cord evenly once it's through. Tie a knot in each end.

5) Turn the cover right side out, slip it over the cylinder or stuffing, and pull the cord taut, gathering the fabric evenly. Tie the ends together and tuck them in the opening.

Covering irregular cushions. To cover cushions of unusual shapes, follow the instructions for box or knife-edge cushions. Make a paper pattern to fit the dimensions of the cushion form. To insure accuracy, test the pattern by making a sample cover from muslin or fabric scraps.

Sewing mitered corners (for knife-edge cushions). You can add a bit more distinction to knife-edge cushions by mitering the corners as shown in the drawing below. Here are two ways this can be done:

mitered corners

1) When the cover is inside out and stitched, fold it so the seams are centered on top of each other and pin the corners. Make the miter by sewing across the corners, perpendicular to the seam lines, 1½" to 3½" in from the corners. (The resulting triangle will determine the cushion's depth.) Trim the corner to eliminate bulk in the seam.

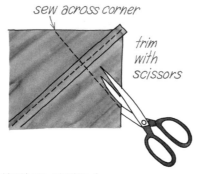

sew across corner

trim with scissors

HOW TO MITER A CUSHION CORNER

2) A folded miter can be made after the cushion cover is sewn and turned right side out. Simply fold the corner inside to make a neat pocket. Because sewing through several thicknesses of bulky fabrics or leather is difficult, this method works best for those materials.

Closing a cushion's opening. As previously mentioned, you have to decide early how you'll close the opening that you push the stuffing through. Install zippers and similar devices according to the directions on the package. If you're inexperienced, putting them in can be difficult; here are a couple of alternatives.

One simple solution is to allow extra fabric at the cushion's backside. From this fabric, make two overlapping fabric panels. Hem and overlap the two pieces 1½" to 3" before stuffing the cushion.

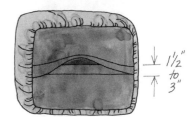

↕ 1½" to 3"

extra fabric at cushion's backside overlaps for an easy-to-make closure

The easiest way to close a cushion is to handstitch the last seam. Of course, to remove the cover, you must cut the seam open. The overcast stitch, shown in the drawing below, is strong, fast, and easy to master.

Another permanent closure is machine topstitching. After the cover is turned right side out and stuffed, fold in the raw edges of the unfinished seam and stitch both together, close to the edge, with a short machine stitch.

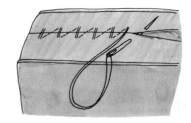

OVERCAST STITCH

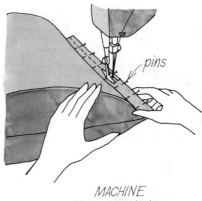

pins

MACHINE TOPSTITCHING

Index